Reality Check

For the past 35 plus years I have had the privilege of serving my clients with dignity, professionalism and success while building a great career. I've also been blessed to have the opportunity to mentor those who shared the passion and desire to raise the bar and make our profession great again.

Reality Check

Lessons Learned, Candor and Consequence

Spyro Kemble

Kemble Books

Copyright © 2018 Spyro Kemble

The moral right of the author has been asserted.

All rights reserved.
No part of this publication may be reproduced, stored in a retrieval system, or transmitted, in any form or by any means, without the prior permission in writing of the publisher, nor be otherwise circulated in any form of binding or cover other than that in which it is published and without a similar condition including this condition being imposed on the subsequent purchaser.

Published by Kemble Books

ISBN 978-1-9866-0978-4

Typesetting services by BOOKOW.COM

Foreword

I am by no means claiming to be the oracle or expert in all things Real Estate. Like many of us, I've had my fair share of lessons that I have both learned and continue to learn as I practice the art of Real Estate. They include industry lessons that have come with the reward of making a quick deal and windfall commission, as well as lessons that have cost me valuable clients, humility (yes, I know how to spell that word) and not to mention compensation.

I know in other industries there are experts that young practitioners can turn to when in need of guidance. Also, in most professions, after obtaining a license, there are mandated continuing education courses designed to keep the licensee at the helm of the latest industry standards.

However, these do not exist in the world of residential real estate. After taking an exam that can be completed in the same amount of time it takes to become a licensed cosmetologist (no insult intended) anyone can get a license to buy and sell real estate, regardless of their prior experience. Unlike other professions, this low barrier to entry leads to hobbyist or part-time dabblers embracing the residential real estate as their newly found career path, which in turn dilutes the credibility of our industry. Not to mention it also lowers the bar of professionalism at the expense of home buyers, sellers and true real estate professionals.

As an immigrant to the United States, I know the American Dream exists. Coming to the United States as a child of a struggling single mother and fast forwarding to today, having sold close to a half billion dollars in real estate to being a cast member on Bravo TV's "Real Estate Wars", and having served as the President of the Newport Board Of Realtors while being a contributing writer for INMAN, I appreciate the value of true work ethic and core values.

As real estate agents, we are given the opportunity of representing or helping acquire one of the most prized possessions of our clients...their home. Therefore, we need to be held to a higher standard of trust and professionalism, by setting a standard, or raising the bar on our industry.

I originally birthed this book exclusively for the real estate profession. I now feel that the thoughts within the book are not only a valuable read for our industry, but for any industry that sells a product or service in a competitive environment, and who needs to examine how we treat the exchange of other people's hard earned money.

I am excited to share this journey with you and show you how easy it is to raise "your bar" and achieve success where so many others fail, regardless of you experience. Most importantly, I am excited to help you identify the agent you want to be, and the agent your client deserves you to be in every facet of the relationship, as you embrace your journey to becoming a better leader in your industry and beyond.

Contents

1	*Negotiate* — Don't *Cut* — Your Commission	1
2	The Common Threads of Great Agents	5
3	Your Personal Brand Image	17
4	"The Price Is Right"… Or Is It?	21
5	The Concierge Realtor	27
6	The Dark Side of Purple	33
7	Is There a Place for EGO in our Profession?	41
8	Just Because you are loud, doesn't make you Right!	45
9	Think Before You Speak	51
10	7 Things You Never Say in Negotiations	57
11	Our Clients Deserve the Best	63
12	Know Our C.R.A.P.	67
13	CIVILITY…Where has it Gone?	71
14	Cultivating Relationships Instead of Real Estate	75
15	The 7 C's of Group Success	81
16	Click Here if You are Not a Robot	85
17	Rising Above the "Hobbyists"	91
18	Check Your Bank Account before You commit!	97
19	Stop Playing Musical Chairs…	103
20	Tales from the Sandbox	109
21	Arm Wrestling with Artificial Intelligence	115
22	Face-off: On What Side of the Desk Do You Sit?	121
23	Honey Badger Don't Care	127
24	Greatness requires fearless obsession	131
25	Choosing Mini-Me	137
26	The "WHO" Behind the Public "YOU"	143
27	Be the Realtor with a "Soul"	147

Sold - Represented Buyer

Location:	Newport Beach, California
Value 2021:	$13,000,000
Lot Size:	3,200 sqft
House Size:	3,619 sqft
Bedrooms:	5
Bathrooms:	5
Garage:	3 car

This property was purchased by my client on a 5 day escrow, (not easy during COVID). The home is located near the world famous "Wedge" bodysurfing spot. Buyer purchased it for a vacation home. His company "Albertson Companies Inc" just went public and its time to come back to his roots as he used to bodysurf here in the 60's.

Chapter 1

NEGOTIATE — DON'T CUT — YOUR COMMISSION

I am a firm believer in knowing your value and being paid for what you deserve. I certainly agree that many of us are fortunate enough to make a good living doing what we do; however, if you have spent years mastering your craft and always putting your clients' needs first, all the zeroes in your commission checks are well earned.

Have I ever cut my commission? Yes. But it was MY choice—and in my 35 years, I can count those times on two hands.

We all know that commissions are negotiable. The commission is negotiated when you take the listing. After that point, it becomes "cutting" —and that is *not* what a luxury agent should engage in.

When a buyer and seller are at an impasse on price, many of us have heard the tongue-in-cheek expression *"we are only a commission away from making the deal,"* as if our paycheck contribution would seal the deal. That was never the deal to begin with.

If a buyer of a multimillion-dollar property needs a portion of your commission to close, they should not be buying that home in the first place. And if you acquiesce, you are selling yourself short.

There is no doubt that as a luxury broker—now more than ever—you need to be a staunch advocate for your clients' needs and expectations. But you also need to apply the same mentality when it comes to your compensation. That is why it's imperative to believe in who you are, believe in what you are, and believe in why you do what you do. Your value is non-negotiable.

As a true professional, your clients deserve the best from you. In return, you deserve to be paid for what you do. That is why one of my work principles is that my value is non-negotiable.

It's important that we differentiate between negotiating your commission and cutting your commission. Negotiating the compensation is done between client and agent prior to signing a listing agreement. It is based on expectations on the client's end and experience on the agent's end. This negotiated amount is what you, the agent, will be working for and will receive when the property closes escrow.

On the other hand, cutting is a unilateral action imposed by the client onto the agent prior to close of escrow—one that was not negotiated and expressly goes against what client and agent agreed to.

In order to have this non-negotiable approach, you must identify what sets you apart from your competitors, also known as your value proposition. What differentiates you from other agents courting the same buyer or seller?

My value propositions are "skillful negotiating" and "strong relationships with other top agents in my area." If you have a good relationship with other agents, deals become less adversary and lead to more win-win transactions for both buyer and seller.

Your value proposition might be that you have a design background, enabling you to stage a home to maximize marketability, or that your sphere of influence is vast, allowing you to expose a property prior to list to selective buyers who want to take advantage of pocket listings. Another value proposition could be that you have exceptional people skills and cater to those clients who require constant communication.

Your value proposition should not be "I can sell your home for 2%"; instead, it should be based on your knowledge of this ever-evolving market (especially in the current health climate), your relationships with other top agents in your area, and your commitment to all aspects of marketing and diligence.

The reality of real estate today is that we used to have to set ourselves apart from other realtors. Now, we have to set ourselves apart from "disruptors," or the discount brokerages who want to change how we do business. But just like a concierge doctor believes his or her value is in service, time, and knowledge, so should you approach your clients with this emotional posture.

Ensure when you are invited for a listing presentation that you focus on your history of success, your value proposition, and your commitment to the seller's goals. Discount brokers/agents who come before or after you will not be able to meet that expectation. Generally, a discount broker's only focus on offering a 1% or 2% seller side commission falls on deaf ears.

The concept of discount brokers like Purple Bricks and others has been tested—and it failed miserably. Don't follow in their footsteps.

Discount brokers focus on quick-in/quick-out deals. Luxury brokers focus on—AND SUCCEED IN—exceeding clients' expectations.

Sold – Represented Buyer/Seller

Location: Bel Air, California
Value 2021: $23,000,000
Lot Size: 2.5 acres
House Size: 7,473 sqft
Bedrooms: 7
Bathrooms: 8
Garage: 6 car

This property was purchased by a famous actress who starred in one of Steven Spielberg's hit movies. The home is located on the Bel Air Country Club. It was also the home that Frank Lloyd Wright the famous American architect resided in.

Chapter 2

The Common Threads of Great Agents

6 Luxury Marketing Essentials You Can't Go Without

I reside in an area called The O.C. The O.C. is a region in Southern California that serves as the center stage for several TV shows. It is draped in designer cars, fashion, sun, surf, sand and some streets are even adorned with luxury real estate mansions. For over 50 years I have called this part of the world my personal and professional home. Over that time, I have seen numerous changes in its culture and perception which has left me with one thing I know for sure: If you are going to stand out in a luxurious part of the world, you need to be exceptional at what you do.

As a luxury realtor with almost a billion dollars in sales, I am often asked how I created a sustainable livelihood in a niche market that some only dream of developing. To which my answer is, "I do it *differently* than one does in the non-luxury market"

If you are someone interested in entering into the competitive luxury market, today is your lucky day because this article will outline what I believe are the six common characteristics required to be a luxury agent in today's market. Six characteristics you need to make your mark, and keep your mark, as a Luxury Market realtor.

Let's begin by qualifying" What is the luxury market?

A Luxury Market is defined as the *Top 10% of all sold values* within that market. For example, my niche luxury market of Newport Beach, California starts at $6,200,000 (10% of all sales are above $6,200,000 as of November 2020). The city of Riverside, California's luxury market, located 45 minutes inland, starts at $675,000. This presents two common sense facts about luxury markets. 1) No matter where in the USA you hang your license, a luxury market exists in your area and 2) No matter what area you practice real estate, there is extreme competition for that luxury market share (the top 10%).

How then do you become the go-to agent for luxury real estate in your luxury market? Here are my 6 pearls of wisdom that help you open that golden gate.

1) Look the Part:

Allow me to start with the least, yet very important aspect of sales, which is appearance. I believe Zig Zigler said it best when he stated, "You cannot climb the ladder of success being dressed in a costume of failure." This means that as a luxury realtor, **look the part.** Believe it or not, it doesn't take much.

For example, some simple secrets include (for men) purchasing a new jacket at least twice a year and tailor your jackets or clothes to fit as though they were meant just for you instead of off the sale rack. Pay attention to the wrinkle factor of your clothing. Linen might be breathable, but it also looks like a hot mess the moment you sit down. Always make sure your socks are new (if you wear socks, which I happen not to), your shoes are clean, and your mani/pedi is fresh. Why? At all high-end showings, you will be shaking hands and likely removing your shoes when touring their prized possession. Always, I mean ALWAYS, arrive in a clean and organized car, with your business card and marketing material presented in an easy to exchange format. A bumbling disheveled realtor does not exude confidence, because as every business mentor will teach you, first impression makes lasting impressions.

2) Know Your Market:

No clothing, grooming nor clean and organized automobile will make a bit of difference in being a top luxury agent if you cannot back-up your image with your experience, knowledge and most importantly results. Selling in a luxury market is so much more than pulling up comparables or placing properties in the MLS with hopes it will sell. ("Hope" by the way, is not a strategy.) No, In the Luxury market, one must bring together a vast number of factors to extrapolate an appropriate list price to in turn, give yourself the best chance of selling your luxury listing. That vast list includes:

- **Knowing your Market Vulnerabilities**: As a luxury agent you need to *know* your market vulnerabilities. This means to be aware of factors that will eventually influence your market such as growing inventory not yet reported in the news, anticipated rate hikes, or pending data that will impact your listing when it shows-up as a comp and it forces you to reduce your price. Not all pending transactions are immediately reported to the MLS, so be vigilant to your market pulse.

- **Knowing Your Inventory:** To adjust, you need to know all the nuances in your market. You need to anticipate trends such as an increase in inventory and a decrease in demand. You need to be well-read by studying all the trade magazines and financial media available. That means making Inman a part of your morning routine as you sip on your first few cups of coffee. This is important because though Real Estate is local, it is still affected by global occurrences.

- **Knowing Your Demand:** Understanding supply and demand is not only basic Econ 101, but it is also critical in evaluating your list price. In The O.C. Luxury market for example, there is currently a market time of 569 days (August 2019.). We have a 6% supply, and only a 1% demand. Based on these numbers it is paramount that your initial list price is strong and that you are prepared to adjust accordingly within the first 90 days, so that your luxury property is not on the tail end of the 569 day cycle, or worse, on the expired list.

- I know all of our clients believe they know more about valuation than we realtors, and as much as I appreciate my clients' input into valuation, I make sure my client has all the pertinent information available so that, together, we can come up with a list price that will give us the best chance of success. If you really want to go the extra mile, retain a luxury appraiser prior to list. This will give you a true market valuation based on tangible and intangible conditions.

- Know the property's luxury features that command luxury prices such as high-end appliances, architectural features, natural resources used throughout, ocean or city views. What does your listing have that is special, unique or rare?

3) Invest in Marketing:

We are all familiar with the business saying, "You need to spend money to make money." I mention that because this is the Golden Rule when it comes to creating your marketing budget. Gone are the days when a 4 – 16-page brochure was enough to sell a luxury home. Now-a-days savvy sellers and buyers expect a lot more including

- **Social Media Presence:** Today's luxury market clientele expects a comprehensive, professional social media campaign, featured on mature social media platforms that meet the target market of your buyer or seller. "No", Snapchat is not a good match for a million-dollar client.

- **Short films or creative videos.** A visual presentation of a luxury home is no longer just a static photo. Search engines like Google now prioritize video and push that content to feeds. Clients should want to showcase their homes on a video platform, which must be shot and edited by professionals, not on your smartphone selfie mode as you peruse through your listing.

- **Virtual Staging.** Not every mansion is decorated properly. Therefore, if you find that your listing is out of date, or that money doesn't buy the taste that it takes to sell your listing, consider Virtual Staging. Virtual Staging allows you to quickly change an out of date look to a Cape Cod or a Contemporary home that will allow a buyer to better evaluate your listing for their lifestyle. Virtual staged photos are now allowed to be featured on the MLS as long as you provide a disclaimer. Virtual staging is not disruptive in cases where clients are still living in the property. Virtually staged photos can also be enlarged and placed on an easel for client walk throughs, allowing prospective buyers to see the potential of the room they are viewing.

- **Staged Social Events:** One way to bring new traffic to your listing and make it an interactive experience is to create a Sunset Cocktail party or other social events for the *who's who* in your area. There is nothing that makes a house more alive to a buyer than inviting them to experience your property with food, entertainment and fun. If people are enjoying themselves at your event, they will talk about it the next day and you will get a great deal of mileage out of this by encouraging photos and sharing on social platforms.

4) Create Luxury Listing Presentations:

You only have one opportunity to make a good first impression. Therefore, if you are fortunate enough to be on a short list of agents being considered for a luxury listing, make sure your listing presentation speaks for your professionalism. For example:

- **Make it Professional**: Without a doubt, make *sure* your listing presentation is professional, detailed and most of all current. The presentation should not only showcase your strengths and sales successes as a realtor, local and international marketing platforms. It also needs to dedicate some page space to the company you represent, as though you are the point-person, because your company is also in the interview queue. Upon completion, both a digital and paper version of the customized presentation should be left with your client.

- **Commit To Memory**: Authenticity is a must, which means that when it comes to interacting with the client, know your presentation and commit your material to memory. So, rather than read the pages like a schoolteacher teaching English, you instead confidently delivery your story, all while observing your client's reaction so you can take pause on the areas, they find

- **Strengths In Numbers**: I have been in this business for 35 plus years. Although I know my "stuff", I never hesitate to ask some key members in my company to attend important presentations with me. That can include the Chief Marketing Officer, who can explain to the client all the resources you have available at your fingertips to market to potential homebuyers. Or my personal favorite, the

President of the Company; which in my case is our owner, Gary Legrand. As the President of our company and a former, uber-successful agent, he not only speaks our language and improves my chances of obtaining the listing, but his presence shows the client that we as a company care from the top down. Together, we show our real estate knowledge for the area as well as the power of the relationships our company has with high net worth individuals who can afford luxury listings.

5) Know the Different Personality Types:

In life, success and failure often comes down to effective communication. Each of us processes information differently, therefore, observe the personality of your clientele.

- **Asses Who You Are Speaking With**: When it comes to being heard, watch the communication style of your client then adapt to their communication style. Meaning, if they are quiet communicators, communicate quietly. If they are colorful communicators, communicate colorfully. If they are direct communicators, communicate directly.

- **Learn to Listen**: Many problems in our industry arise because of our inability to listen. In a day and age where our attention span has dwindled to a mere 8 seconds, we are programmed to get *our* point across as quickly as possible. To be an effective realtor however, you must learn the art of listening. This means close your mouth, open your ears and absorb the hopes, dreams, desires and needs of your luxury client. I like to live by the words of educator Peter Drucker: "The most important thing in communication is hearing what isn't said."

6) Build Relationships:

Finally, when it comes to the Luxury market, nothing is more paramount than the art of cultivating and servicing your relationships. To create sustainability, never forget that when it comes to buying and selling luxury homes, you are dealing with one of the most important assets a person owns. Therefore, treat each deal, both pre and post, as though it is as important to you as it is to them.

So, if you want to be part of the 10% that occupies the Luxury market, make sure you are exceptional in every aspect from looking the part to cultivating your relationships and all things in between, and you will fire on these 6 cylinders.

Sold – Represented Buyer

Location:	Newport Coast, California
Value 2021:	$17,500,000
Lot Size:	13,800 sqft
House Size:	8,800 sqft
Bedrooms:	4
Bathrooms:	6
Garage:	Four car subterranean and one car above

Fastest Escrow ever over $10,000,000. My buyer walked in, looked around on a Monday and had closed escrow on Thursday. The house took four years to build at a cost of approximately $1,200/ft. Most of the material used in the construction of this property was imported from Italy and France.

Chapter 3

YOUR PERSONAL BRAND IMAGE

(3 Steps to Your Physical Who)

As far back as my UCLA days, I understood that my personal image was a brand: A brand that consisted of a popped Polo collar, carefree jock and frat boy who lived beyond his means by dining at the Beverly Hills Polo Lounge while other guys my age went to dinner at Fat Burger or the local pizza joint.

My childish ways of living beyond my means and caring too much about my waist size and tan was almost 40 years ago. But to this day, like a branded cow, some of my college buddies still painfully remind me of that image. It just goes to show *how* we physically present ourselves creates a lasting impression.

In today's world we hear a lot about the importance of our branding. But what do we specifically mean when we say our "Personal Brand Image?" Does our Personal Brand Image help or hurt us when our clients look at the options available to them?

A Personal Brand Image is a combination of who you are (your character and personality), how you present yourself (your physical image) and those to with whom you associate (the brokerage you work for). Without sparing words, it is the shallowness, yet importance of our first impression, and how in our industry, that impression transfers into trust, sustainability, and most important to us, referrals.

Character and Personality: One of the best clarifications of personality and character in business that I have heard states that "Personality is the temperament and traits you were born with, and character is your ability to manage your temperament and traits when stressed." In Personal Brand Image management, this means being aware of how your personality presents itself in first impressions, i.e. your smile, your eye contact, and your body language, as well as how you *manage* the stressful moments and transactions of your daily business. In other words, this means that if by nature your personality prompts you to be angry about something, your character will override that anger and be the fuel, or the break, that determines how your anger will manifest itself.

Physical Image: Marilyn Monroe once said, "I don't mind making jokes, but I never want to look like one." She of all people knew the connection between your personal image and success.

I realize in the sensitive climate we now live, in spite of how we don't like to think that we are judged by our first impression, the fact of the matter is that we are. In our business, the way we look can reflect the type of homes we sell, the level of professionalism we have, and the quality of our business practices. When it comes to image brand management, it is your responsibility to examine your physical image and determine what message your brand is communicating about you.

Your Associations: As a real estate professional, who you associate with professionally is as important as what you put on in the morning for work clothes. Meaning, is your image a reflection of the company or are you your own brand within the company? The answer needs to be, "both."

When I had my reality show on Bravo (I realize that the term 'reality show' is an oxymoron) I made sure that my role was one that was congruent to my brand and who I am.

As our industry continues to evolve itself into an A.I., discount brokerage on line industry, our "human element" will become a more valuable commodity. Part of that human element is to become aware as to who you physically show up as in business and make sure our clients have a reason to retain us for all their real estate transactions.

It's also imperative to consider whether you need assistance in "managing your image" to ensure you are communicating what you intend to. This could range from hiring an agency to help construct your online presence which can include your social media, to hiring a wardrobe consultant to help you dress for success as the saying goes. My agency, Sterling Public Relations, has helped me ensure I am staying true to my brand and what I want to communicate.

At the end of the day, we may not want people to judge a book by its cover, but often they do.

Sold – Represented Seller

Location:	Newport Coast, California
Value 2021:	$13,500,000
Lot Size:	21,359 sqft
House Size:	10,500 sqft
Bedrooms:	6
Bathrooms:	6
Garage:	8 car Subterranean

This property was going through a challenging divorce and every showing there was always a good chance that the parties would act out in public something that no one should ever be a witness of. At one point I thought about handing out hard hats prior to entering the property.

Chapter 4

"The Price Is Right"... Or Is It?

6 Steps to Successfully Price Your Listing

The Price Is Right is a familiar game show where contestants view a consumer product, and then try to guess the actual retail price. The winner of this guessing game is the one who comes closest to the actual retail price.

If only assessing the value of your newest listing was that easy. Professional realtors struggle with the art of finding that right price and selling the home quickly versus losing the buyer because you simply overvalued.

On a personal note, I am no stranger to overbidding and losing the grand prize. I'm reminded of the time when I was in Junior High School and the Sadie Hawkins dance, (an event where the girls ask the guys to the dance) was announced. Four weeks prior to the dance, not short on self-esteem or inflated-ego, with every invite, I kept saying "No" because I was hoping or thinking I could do better. Well, the dance came and went and due to my emotional guessing, I ended-up on my couch watching the Fonz on TV. All because I over valued myself, I never attended the dance, and most likely missed out on a very memorable experience.

So how does that story relate to real estate? It relates because pricing a luxury or complex property is extremely sensitive, challenging and important because if your list price is not rooted in accurate comps that are based on current market conditions and a proper assessment of the demand for that product, you and your client might still be looking for that elusive buyer six months later, and be left chasing a market that is stagnant at best and declining at worst.

As my good friend and boss Gary always says, "You can't sell what you don't have." Meaning you first must secure the listing in order to be able to sell it.

The question then becomes *how* do you set a proper list price that will both satisfy your seller and attract qualified buyers? You find that magic number in the 6 steps to pricing a new listing:

1: Push the envelope, but have a plan "B" in place

When it comes to listing a house, you must be aware of the fine line between "priced to sell" and "priced to keep." To find that fine line you must understand that our properties are not an income property where you take the income minus the expenses, divided by the sales price (or list price) and then come out with a CAP rate that should make it move. Instead, we are dealing with a more subjective sale where many factors are rooted in many subjective parts and opinions. Therefore, when it comes to pushing the envelope, I subscribe to the theory that its okay to price a property 10% above market just to see if the property could produce a buyer willing to pay more than the market bears. That said, you can push the envelope only if two factors are in place. 1) You need to obtain at least six months to a one-year listing, where you can take the first two months of the listing period to see if a potential buyer exits. 2) You must have an agreement upfront with the seller that if no offers come in within the first 60 days (and you do your job of marketing) the list price gets modified closer to your original list price suggestion and the current market condition.

Reality Check: Don't price your property to "keep" it, otherwise you will be like the Maytag repair man and sit at the office waiting for the phone to ring and no one will be calling.

2. Think "Multiple"

Every listing agent's goal is to wake-up in the morning and find multiple offers in your inbox. They might all very well be below the list price, but with every offer you are now able to send out multiple counter offers that will certainly assist in bringing out every buyer's bottom line. The think multiple technique works because eventually the market itself will tell the seller (and you) what the "market value" is, by the offers you receive. So how do we get these multiple offers? The answer is by pricing it just a little under market to get buyers' attention and give them a reason to make the offer right from the start when the listing is new and hot. We all want to connect the dots from "offer" to "acceptance" to "close", but first we must have an offer to start connecting dots to.

Reality Check: Creating a demand up front will ensure the best possible outcome in the end.

3. No "Fake" or False Data

Someone once said that there are three types of lies: Lies, damned lies and statistics.

Many agents pull or rely on comps or data from sales that have no relevance. Though some information might seem accurate on the surface, an app or a website like Zillow or Trulia that pulls an approximate value for a listing in a tract that is made up of cookie cutter homes with very little differences is no gauge for truth. Luxury market or custom homes with the same size home and lot could have a 20% variance in value due to finishes, view orientation and outdoor lifestyle. Which these nuances are mostly only known to local realtors who are entrenched in the market and who have the ability to accurately assess the market.

Reality Check: Don't be robotic in your assessment of value. Your client didn't hire a robot or app.

4. Avoid Monkey See, Monkey Do

When it comes to finding the best price listing for you client don't fall into the Monkey See Monkey Do syndrome. It is very important that you price your listing based on what you believe is the best price, not what other active properties are listing. Just because another agent has a similar listing with very similar characteristics at $5 million and it has been on the market for six months, doesn't mean you price your listing at the same price or more (especially when your instincts and expertise tell you it's worth only $4 million). Many neighbors try to one-up each other when multiple homes are on the market, believing their home is worth more. According to Steven Thomas (Quantitative Economist) 44% of the entire active listing inventory in Orange County has reduced their asking price at least once in the fall of 2018. That was 2018, but sellers still need to be price sensitive and aware of current market trends even with a market that has limited inventory as we have now in 2021. Buyers realize that quality listings are in short supply but they are educated and will not overpay when it comes to unrealistic list prices.

Reality Check: Don't rely on an app or sites like Zillow or Trulia or your seller to determine the eventual list price. Extrapolate from all data and information available to you, including your gut instinct to come up with a list price that will help you reach your seller's goal (hopefully within YOUR listing period)

5: Be Proactive vs. Reactive

Our market is in a constant flux. Interest rates rise, demand falls. Demand falls, prices become stagnant. When stagnation hits, a need for creative and innovate marketing, as well as proactiveness must happen before the other properties in the area make the same adjustments. With limited demand, market time substantially increases and unless you are being proactive, your listing might not sell during your listing period leaving the second or third listing agent in line to save the day.

Reality Check: Don't be the kid who plays musical chairs and when the music stops has no chair to sit in. Be the property that all other listings adjust to.

6. Be prepared to walk away from a listing that you cannot perform.

As I mentioned earlier, I have no problem with taking a listing that is 10% above my BPO or assessment of the market. However, there will be times when you and the seller will be too far apart in agreeing on a list price to anticipate a positive outcome and your best course of action will be to simply walk away. In the end, there will be two disappointed and frustrated people. You, for spending all your time and resources on a listing that did not sell, and the seller for wasting valuable market time with zero results. Trust me: they will blame you for a missed opportunity and not performing as promised just like you will blame the seller for not allowing you to make the necessary adjustments to get it sold.

One of my favorite sayings is, "Be the first born, the second spouse and the third listing agent." When a seller is on his third listing agent they most likely have endured two listing periods where they listed the property too high for it to have any chance of selling.

Reality Check: Know when the best option might be to walk away.

The strategy for proper price listing is by no means a case where "build it and they will come". Or in our case, "list it and they will buy". We as professionals cannot just throw out any list price that the seller might suggest due to their on-line, late night research or their input from other competitors trying to get the listing.

As professionals, we have to be accurate, truthful and insightful in determining a list price that will give everyone the best chance for a desirable outcome.

Sold – Represented Buyer

Location:	Corona Del Mar, California
Value 2021:	$13,500,000
Lot Size:	11,000 sqft
House Size:	6,300 sqft
Bedrooms:	4
Bathrooms:	4
Garage:	6 car Subterranean

The site of my wedding ceremony…direct steps from your backyard to the beach. One of my favorite locations in Orange County.

Chapter 5

THE CONCIERGE REALTOR

(7 Steps to Elevate Your Brand)

Last year Tracy and I were notified by our general practitioner that she was going into "Concierge Medicine." This change meant that if we wanted to remain under her care, we would have to pay a steep annual fee of $5,000 per couple.

My wife, Tracy, and I discussed this recent development. As much as we loved this doctor's personal touch and short notice availability, we felt that at this stage of life it was an unnecessary expense. We couldn't have been more wrong.

As soon as we transferred to a more affordable doctor, our patient care became a cluster of frustration. This included the following: a misread on an important test, long waiting periods for scheduling, multiple wrong diagnoses, zero follow-up on test clarifications, and a consistent bedside manner that was literally on a timer.

It took only ten months of patient-care neglect when we finally abandoned our "money-saving mission," paid the Concierge fee and, like the Prodigal Son, returned to the flock where we were reminded exactly what caring and service is all about.

Please note that the intent of this chapter is not to discredit our interim doctor. In defense of him, he and his staff were very kind; however, both he and his staff lacked the one thing we need when dealing with things personal to us—the people skill of being present.

If you are wondering how my Concierge Medicine story relates to the world of real estate, it is this: our industry is in a transition where discount agencies are investing a great deal of money to convince our clients to jump ship in exchange for a reduced commission. All the while, we agents are on deck with shaky sea legs, wondering just how many clients will abandon the deck to save money. But, luxury agent, it is not our time to worry. I say that because if you are not familiar with the business model of discount real estate, allow me to explain how it works so you can find your "emotional legs" during this somewhat confusing transition in our industry.

Discount agencies such as *Purplebricks* fish for new clients by trying to "hook" potential home sellers with a reduced and set commission in exchange for their services. That formula might be doable for the low end of the housing market. But clearly, it does not work for the luxury market or, for that matter, any listings over $500,000. Here is why: *Purplebricks* advertises a $3,600 listing commission to its selling clients. If you use the average Newport Beach, CA, luxury home price of $4,000,000, a sale that nets a $100,000, 2.5% average commission to the listing agent, you can see that the $3,600 "commission deal" is an impossible number to properly service a listing in all its required aspects. If you question that statement, just take a look at your latest 4 to 16-page marketing brochure, your video montage invoice, or your luxury online digital campaign placement fee, and you will see that the numbers don't make sense.

The question then becomes, where or how does *Purple Brick* or other discount firms make their money? The answer is that they also represent the buyer, which makes up the deficit of the "discount fee" via the additional 2.5% (i.e., $100,000 commission). As we all know, this means double, ending the deal, and becoming a dual agent. This is nothing short of a slippery slope because, suffice to say, you cannot represent both clients' best interests. Obviously, you cannot represent the seller who is paying you to obtain the highest and best price for his/her home and the buyer who is also expecting you to obtain the lowest and best price for him/her.

In this chapter I don't have time to discuss the slippery slope or the many other compromising factors the discount brokerage business module encompasses (see my next chapter, "The Dark Side of *Purple*...."). I can, however, assure you that even when our clients "drink the discount Kool-Aid" and jump ship for only $3,600, as long as there are houses to sell, there will still be clients in the market who want the personal service and presence that only we can offer; that is, if you make the switch to being a "Concierge Realtor."

I know that you must have never heard the term "Concierge Realtor." But that is what those of us who care, who are available, and who are present, are and have always been: an all-hands-on-deck realtor who, just like a Concierge doctor, is available to his/her clients, and won't have to see hundreds to make a profit. Instead, he/she can focus on a few and make sure their needs are met in every way.

As someone on the receiving end of making the mistake of "drinking the discount Kool-Aid," as well as learning the valuable lesson of "you get what you pay for," I will never again question or begrudge my concierge doctor for placing a value on his or her time. Likewise, we authentic real estate professionals do not need to apologize for the value we also bring to the real estate deal to best service our client.

If you are curious how to step into the role of becoming a Concierge Agent, below are my 7 steps to success.

Seven Steps on Becoming a Concierge Agent:

1. **Be Available.** The first step on becoming a Concierge Agent is to make yourself available. That means taking phone calls, even at inopportune times, and returning emails promptly. That also means remaining in constant communication with your client so he/she feels your presence and knows he/she is important to you.

2. **Be Present.** This means to stay aware of the needs, fears, apprehensions, and desires of your client every step along the path of the house-purchasing or selling journey.

3. **Stay Focused on Your Service (not the commission).** *Purplebricks, Help-U-Sell* and other discount brokerages focus on the commission associated with selling a property. They make up loss in compensation by striving to be a dual agent. As a Concierge Agent, your job is to focus on the service and caring aspect of the transaction.

4. **Be Well-Equipped.** This means you must have your storage tank of knowledge full and contemporary. You should know your market inside and out, be current on all of the latest marketing tools available to you. Furthermore, make sure you have great relationships with other local realtors who will want to work with you and strive for the same goal—sell your clients' properties.

5. **Be Patient.** This means remembering that clients can be finicky; therefore, never put them on a purchase time clock.

6. **Operate your Business with an all-hands-on-deck Mentality.** This means to put your maximum effort into your business as the industry continues to shift and change into something new to all of us.

7. **Know Your Value.** The reality of real estate today is that we used to have to set ourselves apart from other realtors. Now, we have to set ourselves apart from "disruptors" or the discount brokerages who want to change how we do business. But just like a Concierge doctor believes his/her value was in service, time, and knowledge, so should you approach your clients with this emotional posture.

As the market place continues to move into a whole new world now more than ever before, it is important to believe in who you are, believe in what you are, and believe in why you do what you do. As a true professional, you deserve to be paid for what you do, and your clients deserve the best from you when they write that well-earned compensation check.

First-rate service and up-to-date information=top-rate client compensation.

Sold – Represented Seller

Location:	Laguna Beach, California
Value 2021:	$12,500,000
Lot Size:	12,197 sqft
House Size:	4,000 sqft
Bedrooms:	4
Bathrooms:	3
Garage:	3 car

Seller owned one of the largest grocery store chains in California. This house and close proximity to the cliff could never be duplicated today due to the stringent coastal requirements.

Chapter 6

THE DARK SIDE OF PURPLE

(Two Depleting and Alarming Facts about Discount Firm "Savings")

I am all for saving money. For instance, I take Uber X when needing a ride to my favorite local restaurant. I buy generic medication at Rite Aid when given the option. And, on occasion, I order the well vodka at my favorite cigar bar. All these things, in my opinion, are not only smart but also have short-term repercussions. After all, if I don't like the car that Uber X sends me, I am in and out in 15 minutes. If I don't feel better with my generic medication, I can buy the brand medication at my next purchase. And, if my head tells me that the well vodka leaves me not feeling so well, I can switch back to Grey Goose at any time.

The same thing cannot be said, however, for hiring a discount brokerage or what I call a Limited Service Brokerage firm. I say that because, as referenced in my most recent article, "The Concierge Realtor," it is our job as professional and experienced Concierge Realtors to commit 100% of our focus to making sure our sellers have the best representation. This means committing to service and capital, working well with other agents by making it as easy as possible to show our listings and, more importantly, encouraging other agents to have their clients make a respectable offer to us.

For all of this, we are well compensated, and I make no apology for it. That is, as we know, in our industry one of the operating expenses that comes out of our paychecks is the costs for us to properly market our properties for sale.

Currently, it is not uncommon to pay as much as half a percent of the list price for the marketing of the property; so be it if you are listing a one million-dollar property that usually exceeds a $5,000 marketing cost, or a 10 plus million-dollar property where the marketing investment can easily cost around $50,000 plus, over a 12-month period. And yes, I said a 12-month period because, in today's market, it would not be wise to take high-end luxury listings for anything less than 12 months due to excess inventory and the extended market time.

That, however, is why I find it offensive when new companies, such as Purplebricks, come along and offer "limited services for a flat fee of $3,600."

What these "seller saviors" fail to tell you is that their enticing fee of $3,600 actually provides a disservice to the seller for two big reasons: 1) The majority of the profits go to the franchise, which in turn leaves the listing agent with a penny- poor budget to properly market the property. 2) The business model of companies such as Purplebricks only pencils out if the listing agents secure their own non-represented buyer to make their commission on the buying side of the deal. This then makes their selling agent a dual agent, a.k.a. a slippery-slope agent.

That leads me to ask a very important question: "How is this savings best for the selling client?" The answer? It certainly is not. At every angle, this "savings" is depleting the seller of proper exposure and available buyers which goes against what we professionals stand for. Let me explain my deep concern over these matters:

Depleted and Alarming "Saving" #1 - Penny Poor Marketing

If you were to put a house on the market back in August of 2018 in my territory of Newport Beach/Laguna Beach, CA, you would be just one of 343 active listings that range between $2,000,000 and $4,000,000. As a Purplebricks' client, it would be impossible to set your listing apart from the other 343 listings on a $3,600 budget. In order to ideally and successfully market a luxury home, you can't cut corners. You must do the following:

1. Run a full page to double truck ad presence (not just a one line, or one of 16 properties on a page) in all of the local magazines and publications.
2. Produce an 8 to 16-page brochure that is mailed out to not only the local residents but also to wealth managers and other top brokerages in your area and surrounding areas.
3. Produce a standalone website with the property address that has an extensive video that tells a lifestyle story, a detailed photo gallery, and all the pertinent details about the property.
4. Maintain a heavy online presence with sites like Zillow, Trulia, Realtor.com,

LuxuryRealEstate.com, etc.

1. Provide a consistent presence on social media, especially Facebook, Instagram and LinkedIn.
2. Implement a digital advertising platform, such as Google Adwords, that exposes your property to buyers who are on sites like the Wall Street Journal, New York Times, Washington Post, Politico, Bloomberg, and others.
3. When necessary, pay for an appraiser when your current price is not moving the property and you need a third-party evaluation to share with your seller.

Now, how can you do all of this for $3,600? Trust me...you can't.

Depleted and Alarming "Saving" #2 – The Slippery Slope of Dual Agency

As I mentioned before, the only way a realtor can make a respectable commission when using companies such as Purplebricks is to secure his/her own buyer. This means the selling agent must now become a dual agent; from the moment an agent steps into this arena, the paradigm of the deal shifts from doing what is best for the selling client (i.e. securing the highest and best offer), to doing what is necessary and best for "me" (i.e. securing any offer as long as they are my clients).

Dual Agency occurs when a single real estate agent represents both the buyer and seller in a real estate transaction. And though Dual Agency Deals create a desirable paycheck by obtaining a full commission, the problem that arises is that a dual agent must be loyal to both the buyer and the seller. But how is that possible if the buyer wants their agent to negotiate for the lowest possible price while, at the same time, the seller wants the highest possible price?

Let me share just four examples to make my point clearer:

1. As the analysis of real estate data is subjective, it can become problematic when you as a seller's agent is looking at a pertinent comp and must advise your sellers of one value and yet, most often you must also advise your buyers of yet another based on the same comp to justify their position on the offer.

2. Your job as an agent is to obtain the highest and best offer for the seller, and at the same time, to make sure your buyer gets the best and lowest price attainable. Whose side do you compromise on to make the deal work?

3. All transactions contain confidential seller information such as the seller's motivation in the deal, his/her financial challenges that might motivate them to sell, their must-sell dates due to a job transfer or closing of another escrow, and their expected bottom-line price that they are willing to sell for. You, as a seller's representative, cannot share this information with your potential buyer as it places your seller in a weakened and harmed negotiating position. The question then becomes, "how do you best protect your seller?"

4. As real estate transactions often require seller's agents to play hardball with a buyer, especially when a buyer submits a request for a reduction in sales price due to deficiencies in the inspection reports, or a market shift happens during escrow, or when repair requests are presented by the buyer in the eleventh hour with the implications that if the seller does not agree the buyer will cancel, how do you save the deal without putting your own interests at heart?

I was recently watching the British Open on national TV when a Purplebricks commercial aired. The commercial showed a man going through a car wash being slapped in the face by the rotating rags. In the midst of his "stupid-man punishment," he had an epiphany where the voiceover said, "The misery you feel when you pay too much in commission and get **nothing** more for your money." The tagline was followed by small print that stated, "Based on estimate aggregate seller savings after payment of market rate buyer commission and Purplebricks seller fixed fee, as compared to the applicable local average commission rate. Projected savings apply to seller transaction only."

As I watched this commercial unfold, I couldn't help but think that its message not only stepped on the lines of "truth in advertising" but, more so, it serves as a total disservice to both of us as professionals and uninformed home buyers and sellers. It is impossible to sell a luxury home on a budget of $3,600. Unlike the commercial wants to have you believe,

Dual Agency is not the smartest representation. The bottom line in discount brokerage or limited service brokerage is that the numbers don't add up, and the service does not show up. Better stated, Uber X is smart savings and Discount Realtor with divided interest is not. How can it be when you are dealing with a person's or family's most substantial asset? It cannot.

Your only job is to make sure you obtain the highest and best results that this market can offer for your seller without the limitations of only selling to "your" clients in order to get paid.

Sold – Represented Seller

Location:	Newport Coast, California
Value 2021:	$10,800,000
Lot Size:	15,000 sqft
House Size:	7,650 sqft
Bedrooms:	5
Bathrooms:	4
Garage:	10 car Subterranean

The subterranean garage can park 10 cars and is 2,800 sqft.

Chapter 7

IS THERE A PLACE FOR EGO IN OUR PROFESSION?

Webster defines EGO as: (noun) The self, especially as contrasted with another self or the world.

Being *all* too familiar with the pros and cons of having an ego, I want to pass on a few observations as to how our ego can serve us and our clients well, or how it can be our own worst enemy in making the deal.

On the pro side of Self, I have always felt that we first must believe in ourselves before we can believe in the home we are selling. Meaning, we must believe in our expertise, our professionalism, our company and in our ability to negotiate the best possible outcome for our clients.

My boss constantly reminds our team that if we can't stand up for our commission in a listing presentation, how can we stand up for the property when we are presented an offer? Well, the belief in oneself allows us to negotiate our worth in the deal and the properties worth in today's market.

> Ego (n): *"The self, especially as contrasted with another self or the world"*

My wife Tracy says that "Awareness is the first step to empowerment." Therefore, as professionals, it's our responsibility to become aware of *how* we show up to the deal. Meaning, do our clients and fellow agents react to our presence with a smile, confidently knowing that a true professional is on their side? Or do they wince and hold their breath until the deal is over?

Reality Check:
Confidence sells and arrogance repels.

If and when however our ego steroids-up on itself, and creates adversary dynamics rather than bringing the buyer and seller together, it's time to reconsider "who" shows up to your listing and who needs to go back into the cage for a time out.

I call this awareness the difference between confidence and arrogance. Or more metaphorically speaking, it's the difference between attracting someone with the scent of your pheromones, or downright offending someone with your Emotional B.O. The question is, what type of agent are you?

We live and work in one of the most beautiful and affluent areas in the world where we are privileged to be representing our clients in their luxury properties. With this privilege comes the responsibility to keep raising our "**bar**" to make sure we not only meet, but exceed our client's expectations.

Sold – Represented Buyer

Location:	Corona Del Mar, California
Value 2021:	$10,000,000
Lot Size:	7,080 sqft
House Size:	5,729 sqft
Bedrooms:	5
Bathrooms:	6
Garage:	3 car

This is the third home for the owner and at 7,080 sqft it is one of the largest lots (triple lot) in Corona Del Mar, ocean side. Approximately 300 feet form the ocean.

Chapter 8

JUST BECAUSE YOU ARE LOUD, DOESN'T MAKE YOU RIGHT!

(3 Ways to be Heard!)

I am half Greek and half German, and when I communicate about something I'm passionate about, there are probably two things you can expect from me:

A) I will believe I'm right;

B) I will probably be loud.

Just ask my wife, Tracy, who is a gentle, strong soul who believes we're all entitled to our own opinion, yet whose opinion I haven't always gracefully embraced.

She, as well as many others, both personally and professionally, have been on the receiving end of what some call my "*Pitbull* Passion." I prefer to call it my "*Point* of Passion," where I state my opinion (which I believe is fact). If the person on the receiving end doesn't meet my wisdom with alliance, I become the Pitbull of repetition, restating my position over and over, only elevating the volume with each reiteration, to make my point more "right!"

Though my ego would like to say my amplified demeanor is commanding the conversation, what has really happened at that moment is that I have lost the *Art of Communication*. The *Art of Communication* is the ability to effectively communicate a message, have it received from the opposite party, have it responded to with proper facts, and then have it returned for a win-win resolve.

Unfortunately, the lost *Art of Communication* is something I am seeing a lot more of in our industry. Recently, as Karma would have it, I was on the receiving end of a Pitbull, when a new agent busted into my office and proceeded to "passionately" lecture me on the value of one of my oceanfront listings. He wanted me to accept his less-than-appealing offer that neither my clients nor I were interested in. Now, keep in mind, I am very supportive of agents offering their opinions of value that I can use to make adjustments, or help the seller be more educated on the market. But, like my wife, I've discovered that, I too, am not a fan of "Pitbull Passion," especially when it is:

A) Unsolicited;

B) Uneducated;

C) Not fact-driven.

Reality Check:
Communication is only effective if the receiving party can hear it, and hearing has nothing to do with volume.

The incident with the "passionate" new agent reminded me of something my college professor always impressed on us as students, which was the importance of **"owning"** a position in a debate. His rule of thumb was to "make sure your position is rooted in facts and always articulated in a polite and civil manner."

So, in the realm of the *Art of Communication*, what does "owning" your position look like in the throes of negotiation? Below are three steps to success.

Three Steps to Success:

1. **Listen, listen, and listen!**
   Most people in negotiations make the mistake of formulating their comeback, before their client (or spouse) has even finished their sentence. The *Art of Communication* remembers that "a closed mouth means open ears." This means, if you can learn to hear the *need* of the person in front of you and *address* that need, you are already one thousand steps ahead of the game.

2. **Know your facts and recognize your opinions.**
   The late U.S. Senator, Daniel Patrick Moynihan, said it best when he was quoted as saying, "Everyone is entitled to his own opinion, but not to his own facts." As much as you might not want to admit it, there's a possibility that you may not be the oracle to all.
   In the real estate business, it is not enough to think you are right. You must show up with the facts and BE right. At the same time, it is okay to simply have a personal opinion. Your job as the agent for the buyer or seller of your deal is to know the difference, and to make sure you properly communicate it.

3. **Stay Focused on the End Goal.**
   The end goal to the *Art of Communication* is to have all parties reach a win-win. This is *how* we close deals, my friends, but they can only happen if the wall of miscommunication remains down. As a lead negotiator, your job is to manage your communication style with finesse. This means maintaining polite dialogue between the clients and all agents, even those who don't know what they are doing. This means actively listening to hear the needs of those with thin skin in the game. This especially includes keeping down the volume (and all caps on emails) when things get passionate.

As a man and as a Real Estate Broker who is constantly working on raising my personal bar of professionalism, I am learning to tone down my

Pitbull Passion. This has been one of the best personal and professional lessons I've embraced. It has taught me that being louder doesn't make me right. I have learned that my German mother's rule, "Keep politeness at all costs," is a must! Negotiating a deal is an emotional game, and it has taught me that my Greek passion and volume is best reserved for the "Opa and Ouzo," rather than for the client, co-worker, or spouse.

May low-volume negotiations be with you!

Sold – Represented Buyer/Seller

Location:	Laguna Beach, California
Value 2021:	$8,700,000
Lot Size:	6,175 sqft
House Size:	5,000 sqft
Bedrooms:	5
Bathrooms:	6
Garage:	3 car

The owner is a former Wimbledon Singles Champion. The property is located behind the gates of an exclusive private beach community.

Chapter 9

THINK BEFORE YOU SPEAK

(5 Steps to Curing the Open Mouth Syndrome - or aka, becoming a Better Listener)

I was born with a limited filter. Meaning, when it came to speaking my mind, I suffered from what I call the "Open Mouth Syndrome." Just ask my wife Tracy who has joked about the number of times she has wanted to body slam my unfiltered words as they exited my mouth and steam-rolled into the ears of bystanders.

Over the years, I have diligently worked on closing my Open Mouth Syndrome, and slowly I have been able to apply a stop process that has helped me both professionally and personally. For instance, in my personal life, I no longer meet Tracy's difference of opinion with an aggressive retort, but rather try to engage in empathetic dialog. In my professional life, I have learned to allow my brain to process information prior to generously donating loud articulations. The outcome has been nothing short of magical in that my relationships both personally and professionally are much more prosperous.

In this chapter, I plan to share the emotional medicine I used to treat my Open Mouth Syndrome. But before I do, let's see if you too suffer from the condition that can negatively affect both your career and personal life! Below are a few questions to ponder...

The Open Mouth Syndrome Test:

Have you...

[ ] had listings get cancelled by a Seller because he (or she) felt that they were not being heard?

[ ] fumbled offers because both agents thought they were listening when they really failed to hear what was being said?

[ ] lost partnerships because someone failed to hear the needs of the other and added fuel to the fire by saying things they later regretted?

[ ] lost new promising agents because your mentorship skills were more focused on the mistakes of a new agent (most likely caused by their lack of knowledge), rather than listening to their newbie questions and taking the time to be a mentor?

[ ] believed, that since you are an expert in your territory, this makes you the oracle of all things real estate related?

[ ] had personal relationships suffer a slow death because you were too busy thinking of a comeback or point of view, rather than listening to the needs of the most important people in your life? (This is one that I was personally guilty of in my relationship with my wife, Tracy for years.)

Reality Check:
Listen and Silent are created from the same letters.

If you find that you suffer from the Open Mouth Syndrome, I have an easy remedy for you. It comes from the advice of our founding President, George Washington who wisely said, "Think before you speak." Though he didn't know it at the time, President Washington was speaking on something that today we call "active listening," which is the art of hearing the other person first, before responding in conversation. If you are curious what active listening looks like, examples include learning to hear "why" a client is selling or buying their house before you pitch them your brand. Or, it's learning to hear the point of view of an agent who is presenting a less-than offer, rather than dismissing them instantly. Or, it's learning to have good bedside manners to our "back seat driver" clients who are practicing real estate without a license by trying to tell us how to do our job. Or, as the late Attorney Donn Kemble, my father and mentor, would say to me as we would smoke our cigars and drink our cognac together, "Son, if a person wants to say the moon is made out of cheese, don't waste your breath arguing your point. Just ask them, "And what kind of cheese would that be?" He never had the need to show how smart he was or belittle a person by pointing out how absurd they were. He instead taught me these five simple steps to becoming a better listener listed below.

The Five Steps to Becoming a Better Listener:

1. **Listen with Silence:**
   The first step to becoming a better listener is learning the art of silence. As I mentioned earlier, *Listen* and *Silent* are anagrams, meaning they are words made up of the same letters. Therefore, when someone speaks, close your mouth, open your ears, and simply listen to what they have to say.

2. **Be Present:**
   The second step in the art of listening is making the effort to be present. In this day and age of over stimulation, smartphone distraction and preoccupation keep us from being present to the person in front of us. The rule of thumb to being present is to remember that our presence is a present to those we encounter.

3. **Expand Your Viewfinder:**
   The third step in the art of being a better listener is to remember that difference is what makes the world go around. In other words, be open-minded to various points of view, especially the ones that don't align with yours. It is easy for all of us to focus on our own needs and dismiss the input of others. But when we do this, we run the risk of missing the essence of what is behind the communication of the other party. It might not be your cup of tea, but then again, you might just learn an unexpected lesson along the journey.

4. **Take a Breath and Don't be Immediate:**
   One of the biggest mistakes we make in poor listening is to respond too quickly. In fact, not every issue requires an immediate answer. Most issues are to be analyzed before you respond verbally or in writing.
   My father, who was also an attorney, said it best when he would advise me, "Spyro, assume that anything you say in writing, a Judge will read back to you one day in court." What he meant is, "never respond in haste and say things that you might regret one day." Or, in other words, "learn to argue both sides of the issue in your head before you respond out of your mouth!"

5. **Take "Ego" out of Communication:**
   In communicating, there is something called, "emotional arm wrestling," where *winning* is more important than *resolving*. The final step to becoming a better listener is to wisely choose your battles. This means to determine if you want to be right, or if you want to make the deal work. Sometimes it is better to let the other agent connect the dots of the deal and allow them to come to the conclusion at hand, leading you both to a win-win deal for the client.

It has been said by world leaders and relationship experts that "The greatest human handicap is a breakdown in communication." My belief is that this fracture can be repaired by learning the art of listening and the simple century old gift of learning to think before we speak. It is the cure to the Open Mouth Syndrome that will not only open the door to better clients and better deals, but most importantly to me, to becoming a better spouse.

Make it a point to touch someone's life today with the gift of active listening.

Sold – Represented Buyer

Location:	Newport Coast, California
Value 2021:	$8,800,000
Lot Size:	20,375 sqft
House Size:	7,300 sqft
Bedrooms:	5
Bathrooms:	5
Garage:	4 car

The buyer purchased it unseen. Just a video and photos. Closed in 15 days. To this day I have never seen or met the buyer.

Chapter 10

7 THINGS YOU NEVER SAY IN NEGOTIATIONS

Back in my high school days (circa 1976), one of our favorite things to listen to was a monologue by George Carlin called "The Seven Words You Can't Say on TV." At the time, there was no YouTube or the Internet, so we listened to this classic piece via a record player or on the Tonight Show where the actual words were bleeped.

For those too young to remember this monologue about the seven words you could not say on TV in 1978, let me say this. It was not only extremely funny, but it was also on point. Forty years later, as I walk down George Carlin memory lane, I'm faced with the reality that when it comes to communicating and negotiating with other agents, we also have seven words and phrases that, as professional realtors, we should never say or put in writing.

As oracles of our clients, our job as professional agents is to build a bridge to a buyer's and seller's meeting of the minds and make sure nothing we say will get in the way of making and closing the deal. This Includes not using the seven words or phrases that we need to avoid.

Here is your bleep list:

1. **Bottom Line**
   "What is your seller's bottom line?" If I had a dollar for every time an agent asks me this question, I would have enough money to fund my cigar habit for a few months. Most of us know that our clients don't tell us what their bottom line is because, for the most part, they don't know what their bottom line is. Even if they did, we as agents should never communicate that number! We are paid a great deal of money for what we do, and part of our job is to negotiate; eventually we do come to a point that will make the deal, no matter how many counters it might take.

   <u>Reality Check:</u> Get the offer accepted, one counter at a time. It's not a microwave-type of deal.

2. **"AS IS"**
   This property is being sold "AS IS." If you look at our Purchase Contract you will see that it already states that the sale is AS IS, so why restate the pre-disclosed obvious? Does it discourage a buyer from submitting a request for repair, or worse, open a second round of negotiating? Stating it again will not jeopardize or hinder the deal; however, redundancy is at best not necessary and at worst will make you look less than professional.

   <u>Reality Check:</u> Know your RPA (purchase contract) inside and out and all that it implies.

3. **We**
   "*We* don't think this will work." The last time I checked, this transaction is not about us because of one simple reason. This is not our money being negotiated. We might know what is motivating our client or the "why" behind the sale or purchase. But in the end, only our client can adequately respond to any offer that is before him or her. We are not entitled to have any stake in the transaction other

than representing our client to the best of our ability. Therefore, when it comes to "we", though personalizing is a means to show a front-line unity, we can never cross the line by assuming we always know our client's intentions.

<u>Reality Check:</u> There is no "we" in a real estate transaction…only the "client".

4. **Offended**
   "We are very offended by this offer." This phrase is a dual violator in that "we" and "offend" are in one phrase. Again, why are "you" offended? You as the agent should be ecstatic that you have an offer to be "offended" about, and your client should be jumping for joy that you have secured an offer for them to consider. Without a written offer, we as agents have nothing to negotiate.

   I enforce this statement with a reminder that back in September 2018, 44% of all listed properties in Orange County have had a price reduction. Therefore, what you considered offensive in the beginning of the listing might just cause you to rejoice five months into the listing. What many agents and sellers don't realize is that once a buyer puts an offer in writing and signs it, no matter how low it may be, the chances of buyer and seller coming together have increased drastically.

   <u>Reality Check:</u> You should embrace ANY offer that comes in as it is the gateway to making the deal.

5. **Verbal Offer**
   "My client wants me to make this offer verbally to save time and to get it closed before we put it in writing." Where do I begin? Entertaining or responding to a verbal offer is the best way to negotiate against yourself. Has it worked at times with certain agents that you have a very close relationship with? Maybe. But more often than not a verbal offer is a disaster in the making. Our broker of record, John B, always says, "If it's not in writing, it doesn't exist or

didn't happen, unless it can come back to hurt you".

<u>Reality Check:</u> Don't ever negotiate against yourself; you will lose."

6. **Emotional Responses**
"**Your Client is a Moron.**" Even the kindest of us have wanted to say this at one time or another. The least professional of us have blackened our standards by putting it in an email. When it comes to irritating clients, cooler heads prevail.

Just like a marriage, responses rooted in name-calling emotions will most likely not seal the deal. As a professional realtor, you are to serve as a filter between the outside world and your client. As such, it is not your place to pass forward every inflammatory comment that the agent of the other client might pass on to you.

My father, who was a real estate attorney and the smartest man I knew, once said to me, "Be careful what you put in writing; always do so with the knowledge that one day a judge might read it back to you."

When it comes to effective communication, you and the other agent are on the same side. You are both sharing in the commission paid by the seller; treat each other with respect.

<u>Reality Check:</u> If it is not material to the deal, keep it to yourself.

7. **Offer via email**
"**I will email you the offer.**" One word comes to mind when I hear this – "lazy."

As a professional realtor whose job is to present offers to real-life clients, why would you put the success or failure of the deal in the hands of the other agent? They can never articulate your client's position and point of view better than you. Therefore, if you are given the chance, ALWAYS present your offer in person to the other client. If you are representing the buyer, ALWAYS get in front of the seller and communicate the "why" behind your offer. On the flip side, if you are representing the seller, always encourage the other agent to present in person; this way the onus is not on you, but on them, to be the carrier of sometimes not-so-good news when it comes to the expectation of the seller.

<u>Reality Check</u>: Don't let anyone else speak for you or communicate your client's intent.

As my walk down memory lane comes to a close, allow me to mention that I know the above words and phrases can be counter-productive in business because over my 35-year career I have used each and every one, and not just once. I have learned the hard way that none of these have any place in a successful and smooth transaction and if anything can keep us looking unprofessional or worse, it would be losing a deal.

The next time you are negotiating for your client, remember that navigating through a transaction successfully is often a journey through a minefield; it takes sophisticated communication skills, calm demeanor and just plain common sense. As a friend of mine always says…use your common sense. It's free.

Sold – Represented Buyer

Location:	Corona Del Mar, California
Value 2021:	$8,200,000
Lot Size:	8,800 sqft
House Size:	6,520 sqft
Bedrooms:	5
Bathrooms:	5
Garage:	3 car

The property features a 600-bottle wine cellar and has access to private beach.

Chapter 11

OUR CLIENTS DESERVE THE BEST

I attended a California Association of Realtors meeting in Indian Wells, and I must confess, there were a few things above my pay grade, and many below my level of interest or caring...

However, there was one take-away that confirmed my on-going conviction, which centered around the bar we set (or lower) for our industry. The meeting helped set my focus on the issue of "Open Borders" in the real estate licensing process, and what we need to do to ensure that only the most qualified of applicants obtain a license to represent clients that expect the best of us.

Reality Check:
The entrance may not have demanded the best of you but your clients most certainly do.

The Need to "Raise the Bar": During the meeting, an amendment was presented that required a vote. The amendment called for a change in the current Real Estate License testing that would give the "tester" the ability to take the state agent exam three times (instead of twice), before a three-month waiting period is enacted.

As someone who is passionate about the state of our profession, I feel if you can't pass a simple real estate test, do you really have the right to be trusted with your clients most important assets? I say "No."

Currently, the bar is set relatively low when it comes to obtaining a license in our field, and the end result is the pool of quality agents keeps getting diluted. There are too many licensed agents who currently treat our profession as a hobby or a part time job.

> **Profession (n):** *"A calling requiring specialized knowledge and often long and intensive academic preparation"*

Other entities such as The California Bar Association, only offer their exam twice a year. They do this to protect the level and expertise of law practitioners, which ultimately protects the clients. If our goal is to raise the standard of our industry, I believe we can learn from their example, and protect how easy it is to enter our industry.

Being a Realtor is a privilege and a profession. It is not a right or recreation. It is certainly not a hobby. Nor is it something to "do on the side." Instead, Real Estate is a multi-billion dollar industry that is dealing with contracts, law, finances, psychology, emotion and not to mention the most precious purchase a person will ever make. It is a respected profession that we need to treat and protect as such. And that is why changing the test guidelines is not a good idea.

As someone once said, "Suck it up buttercup, not everyone gets a trophy." This must also include practicing Real Estate, because not only do our clients deserve better, but so do we as Professionals.

Sold – Represented Buyer

Location: Corona Del Mar, California
Value 2021: $8,100,000
Lot Size: 32,000 sqft
House Size: 7,141 sqft
Bedrooms: 6
Bathrooms: 6
Garage: 5 car

The property features a second structure over the garage that is suited for multi-generational living. That was the main factor why my client bought it. Separation of Church (Mother) and State (Son).

Chapter 12

KNOW OUR C.R.A.P.

To "Raise our Bar" we must Know our C.R.A.P.

BEFORE you get offended, let me explain. As I've mentioned several times, we as Realtors have been given a great opportunity. 1) We are entrusted with the purchase or selling of someone's most substantial asset and lifestyle. 2) We tend to have an excellent compensation package for doing our job. The question then becomes, in exchange for these two luxuries, what is required or expected of us in return? The answer is, to "Know our C.R.A.P." which is a formula I've developed to keep you at the cutting edge in your industry.

Reality Check:
Eat, Sleep and Breath C.R.A.P. if you want to be the best.

C: Competitive – Step one in Knowing your C.R.A.P. is facing the fact that our industry (like none other) is an extremely *competitive* market. Both sellers and buyers have choices, including access to some of the top Realtors in the nation right here in our own backyard, at their fingertips. Your job is to be on your "A" game at all times. This means creating simple disciplines such as going on weekly property tours. Spending time in your office with your fellow agents as they have access to many pocket listings. Checking the daily "hot" sheet. Discovering what is new on the market. Being aware as to what went into escrow or closed. And most importantly, asking yourself "why" did it sell at this price and how does it impact my listing?

> **C.R.A.P. (n): Spyro Kemble** *"the essence of knowledge and applying it"*

R: Real Estate - Besides excellent and professional Customer Service, it is important to remember that what we really sell is *Real Estate*. Therefore, as a Real Estate Professional your job is to *know* your Real Estate. This means knowing how to defend your list price when we are presented with a low-ball offer that makes no sense, or when the appraisal does not substantiate the sales price, or (a more surfacing problem) when the seller presents you a Zillow Estimate (Zestimate) that shows a 30% higher market value than what we know to be true. As a professional, *Real Estate* is your bread and butter. Therefore, to succeed, you must eat, live and breathe *Real Estate* as your finest cuisine.

A: Adjust - In an ever-changing market and an ever-changing *way* of marketing, there is one-character trait all professional Agents and Brokers need. That is, the ability to *Adjust*. Our market is in a constant flux. For example, a hot Spring market turns into a good Summer market, which then turns into a slower Fall, and perhaps a cool Winter. Valuation and pricing is paramount in our industry, and the only way to truly be able to market a property to sell within your listing period, is to know what you are up against; or another word, "Know your Crap" and more importantly, know how to *market* your crap. Every house, like every person is unique. Therefore, find the right media outlet that will best expose your property to the most ideal customer and for Pete's sake follow thru on your marketing commitment ($) you made to the seller.

P: Proactive – The days of placing a sign on the lawn and walk-in buyers making a top of the market offer, have been over for a long time. You must therefore be one step ahead of the game/competition. This means that if you do not receive an acceptable offer within 30 to 60 days of the list price (and you have done your job) *make changes*. For example, retain a professional stager, declutter the property if necessary, add landscaping or remove landscaping, propose a price reduction if you can justify it, and most of all stay on the cutting edge of marketing with all the available tools including virtual staging, videos that tell a story, and international marketing to make sure your clients receive the best possible representation.

It is a competitive world out there. But success in this industry is still achievable as long as you are humble enough to know your C.R.A.P. and take the time daily to eat your fair share.

Sold – Represented Seller

Location:	Newport Coast, California
Value 2021:	$6,700,000
Lot Size:	12,632 sqft
House Size:	6,067 sqft
Bedrooms:	5
Bathrooms:	6
Garage:	3 car

This property was investors owned (REO) and they sold it for less than what was owed. That is a very rare occurrence in our market today as we have less that 1 percent distress properties for sale. A substantial departure from 2008 when the distress rate went from 6% to 20% for Orange County.

Chapter 13

CIVILITY...WHERE HAS IT GONE?

THE other day I was watching TV when suddenly a "comedian" held up a decapitated, bleeding head of the President of the United States. At the same time my wife, who as at an out-of-state speaking engagement, phoned and told me about the tears she encountered while speaking to a group of young college women who risked harm because of expressing a less-than popular view while on campus.

In my continual quest to raise the bar on our profession in 2017, I cannot help but ask, has anyone noticed that civility and respect are disappearing? From how nations deal with one another; to our intolerances of differences to what is "right"; to our social media opposing viewpoints cyber bullying, civility is becoming a lost art in our great country.

The trickle down affects even infiltrate our local market where too often, our communication style amongst fellow agents has turned into a contest of who can send the tougher email.

Reality Check:
Be present, polished and polite.

My question is, how did we get here?

I believe that much of our civility deficiency is attributed to the advancement of electronic communications. We are all guilty of shooting off a text, rather than picking up the phone, or of sending an email with negotiations, instead of meeting face-to-face for lunch. For Pete sake, some of us are even guilty of sending emojis flowers as a thank you gift, instead of taking time to "stop and smell" the real things ourselves!

> Civility (n): "polite, reasonable, and respectful behavior"

So, what can we do to bring back the art of civility to the heart of what we do? I have five recommendations:

1. Meet rather than email: Step one in re-finding civility is to go back to basics. This means, make a point of having one-on-one meetings, as only we can best represent our viewpoint.

2. Pick up the phone: I certainly see the need for creating a paper trail for all material communications. But a personal phone call with discussion and dialogue is still the best remedy to settling any potential pitfalls.

3. Remember the goal is that everyone gets to win. Therefore, allow for a difference of opinions from all parties, without taking it personal.

4. Keep the real estate negotiations between agents. Our clients don't need to hear every sparring move or verbal punch about their property or the deal. As an agent, we are the buffer. And our job is to keep our clients feeling *good* about their house and who their buyers are and any deals that come their way.

5. Live the Golden Rule: Treat others as you would have them treat you. Perhaps by doing so, civility will become a trickle up effect and just by focusing on your own backyard, that energy can affect our personal and professional life, which can then affect a community. Then perhaps a nation. And who knows, it may even impact the world...one can only hope, anyways.

Sold – Represented Buyer/Seller

Location:	Newport Beach, California
Value 2021:	$6,800,000
Lot Size:	22,651 sqft
House Size:	7,652 sqft
Bedrooms:	5
Bathrooms:	8
Garage:	3 car

The seller of the property was once married to ex-wife of the heir to the Marshall Field's estate and produced films from Revenge of the Nerds to Three Men And A Baby, Jumani, Bill & Ted's excellent adventure, Runaway Bride and Beirut among many more.

Chapter 14

CULTIVATING RELATIONSHIPS INSTEAD OF REAL ESTATE

My $200,000 lesson…

I would like to think at my ripe age of 63, I have learned my big lessons in business. But I haven't. Just recently I had a setback, or better stated, an *insight* that made me stop and examine *my* bar, and take a step to raise it.

Here's what happened: I was doing my daily research on properties that have just come on the market and had closed escrow the night before in my neighborhood when I came across a home in Newport Beach that closed escrow for $7.5 million. I wasn't surprised at the price of the home since it came with an unusually large boat dock. I was instead *jarred* to read that the purchase was done by a client of *mine*; or at least I *thought* he was as a client of "mine." And why wouldn't I? I had closed over $20 million dollars in properties for him. The problem was, that was 9 years ago.

Reality Check:
Cultivate and maintain relationships and the real estate will follow.

So, what went wrong? Why did my annual Holiday gift basket, or occasional phone call not keep me on my client's viewfinder? The answer I discovered, was the importance of visibility; specifically, our client's visibility.

In our conversation he said, "Spyro, you have always done an amazing job for me and I couldn't have been happier with how the deals went down. I have made great investments because of your advice, and you have made me a great deal of money. However, in the past 9 years, outside of your annual holiday gift basket and occasional 'Hello', I have had *limited* contact with you. You have never called just to ask how I am doing, or if I have any needs that you can assist me with."

Apparently, while I was busy looking for gift baskets, not only had the other realtor sent him *monthly* market updates, pocket listings in his neighborhood, and even brought him a *real*, unsolicited offer, which in turn got his foot in the door, but he asked one very important question that I failed to ask, which was *"Mr. Client, if you were to ever move from this amazing property (that I found for you and thought was your dream home forever) what would excite you enough to do so?"* My client's response was, "A Bayfront that can accommodate a 75 foot yacht"; that subsequently closed for 7.5 million dollars and earned a paycheck of just over $187,500 for the other realtor.

So, what is the moral or lesson of this story? It is a 3-part "Raise the Bar" lesson that I write more to myself, than to my readers, as a reminder of how to do things better.

> **Relationship (n):** *"the action of making a mental connection"*

1. **Cultivate the Relationship instead of the Real Estate.** In our industry, we certainly have *specialists*, but let's not fool ourselves. We are not necessarily "special." Meaning, the ratio between Realtor

versus client is massive. Therefore, when we get the luxury of representing a client for the purchase of their next home or investment, *make sure you know your client.* Meaning, *know* what makes your client take notice, and *understand* your client's needs and wants, so that *when* real estate comes on the market you will know immediately if it fits in your client's box.

Contrary to what I've heard other agents say, it is *not* about the spin and *putting* your client in a deal. It's about *matching* a deal to your client's needs and wants; which this *awareness* happens only if you have a *relationship* with your client that goes beyond the showing of the properties, emailing new listings, or even Holiday gift baskets.

2. **Celebrate the Relationship After your Deal Closes.** Nine years before my client's latest purchase, I sold him a house on the golf course that was a gem. He and his family were happy beyond belief, and I, as a competent Realtor, was *proud* of my stellar "Realtor" performance. However here was the problem: My short-sightedness told me that I found them their *dream* home. But *never* did it cross my mind to *ask* him what his *next* dream house might look like: Be it then, be it in a year from the sale, or as my lesson taught me, be it 9 years later.

Just because escrow has closed, your relationship with your client has not. As a professional Realtor, your job therefore is to stay connected. Meaning, send your client monthly market updates, birthday wishes for the family, and treats for their dogs when you go back to *visit*. Above all, cultivate a long-term relationship that is built on *genuine* caring. *Visibility,* long after the sale is what will keep you on your client's viewfinder not only as a friend, but as a trusted Realtor who can be called upon to guide and direct them on their next purchase.

3. **Foster the Relationship to Expand your Referral Base.** Marketing and branding is certainly important for a continual and successful pipeline of business. But there is no better formula to securing new

prospects than a referral from a happy and satisfied client. Your existing clients have the power to *transfer their trust*, which is a priceless gem in our industry. We always focus on the transfer of title but instead we should be focusing on the transfer of trust if we want to expand our business.

My very dear friend Paula Steurer (Sterling Public Relations) posed a very interesting question in one of her recent seminars. It was, "What is your WHY?" As I sit on the reality of my very expensive $200,000 lesson, I am reminded that my WHY is *not* just selling real estate, but instead it is building relationships; relationship that will keep my clients visible, and where I meet their personal and professional needs.

Sold – Represented Buyer

Location:	Laguna Beach, California
Value 2021:	$6,900,000
Lot Size:	5,200 sqft
House Size:	4,660 sqft
Bedrooms:	4
Bathrooms:	4
Garage:	2 car

Every level has white water views and if I were to build a house today, this would be it.

Chapter 15

THE 7 C'S OF GROUP SUCCESS

Raising the Bar on Your Group

Recently, the world lost an amazing artist. It was the great Jerry Lewis who was not only a *stand-alone* comedian, but also a member of the great comedic *team,* Lewis and Martin.

As more and more "Groups, Teams and Partners" continue to emerge in our industry, his passing got me thinking about what it takes to create a successful group, versus a facade of scale that could potentially mislead the client.

Without a doubt, some existing Groups are the real-deal. Powerhouse teams with extensive portfolios set a fantastic example of how working in tandem can create a stronger bottom line and quality experience for clients.

Reality Check:
A team working together is far more productive than an individual.

But where does that leave the small agents of two or more, who want to compete with the big boys (or big girls in this case)? Or how can we protect both the client and agent, by making sure the *standards* of a Group are authentically in place?

My answer is, just like hotels have a criteria and star rating for industry standards, I believe we agents need to have a *Group* Star rating, which I call it the 7 C's of Group Success. It looks like this:

> **Group (n):** *A collection of individuals who have regular contact and frequent interaction, mutual influence, common feeling of camaraderie, and who work together to achieve a common set of goals"*

The 7 C's of Group Success

1. **Culture:** To begin, every group needs a culture. In a sense, your culture is your team's personality that separates you from the rest. In other words, it's knowing *who* you are, *what* you represent as a team, and *how* you are going to present and execute yourself on the market, as a group.

2. **Center:** Once your group is formed, it's important to remember that, as the old saying goes, "There's no 'I' in team." For a successful group to collectively stand, there *must* be one professional leader. But forming a *synergy* is as equally important. Therefore, your new back tattoo shall read: A group is *not* a team of individuals who are banned only by your name. A group is a *collection* of people who execute the end-goal of your group's mission.

3. **Communications:** There's nothing worse than hearing a team member say, "I don't know." Therefore, communication is a must within the group. Daily listing update emails, weekly training meetings, or monthly personal cocktails or lunches are all a part of teaching, updating, strategizing and team-building. Remember: People join a group to be *part* of a team. And *all* team members need to feel connected and visible.

4. **Cultivate:** Just like no two fingers are the same, neither are individual members in a group. Therefore, make sure that each of your team members has a specific place and purpose in the team. In addition to that, if you're anything like me, you hate to delegate. But as a leader, it's time to get over it. Learning the art of letting go is the only thing that will make your team stronger.

5. **Creative Open Door:** There are two things I know for certain. Our industry is always changing, and we old guys are getting older. That said, a progressive Group must be open to learning *new* things. Diversifying your group will keep the creative eyes open, and who knows! The next creative genius on how to improve your business might be right underneath your nose.

6. **Commit to Teaching:** As a group leader, there's one mantra you must remember. "People do not know what they do not know." Therefore, *when* a team member makes a mistake (and believe me they will) your job is to become a mentor and a teacher. It's a known fact that people want to be led and taught. And the long-term success of your group will be determined by *how* your team *grows* underneath you.

7. **Client Care:** And finally, in a world where Zillow keeps infringing on our business, the best way to set yourself apart is by *service and professionalism.* In other words, "Client Care." At the end of the day, the success of our business comes down to the *satisfaction* of our clients.

So, if you are thinking about adding the designation of Group, Associates or Partners after your name, make sure you are ready to take on this responsibility, because though reaching that goal, (or the close of the deal) is a personal feel good, "taking it as a team" is *priceless*.

Sold – Represented Buyer

Location:	Encino, California
Value 2021:	$6,700,000
Lot Size:	17,400 sqft
House Size:	8,400 sqft
Bedrooms:	6
Bathrooms:	7
Garage:	3 car

The owner played for the LA Lakers. It was worth traveling up to Encino for this deal. I had to keep telling myself this after a two hour 405 commute.

Chapter 16

CLICK HERE IF YOU ARE NOT A ROBOT

Raising the Bar on Our Relatability

RECENTLY, I logged on to an online shopping website and before checking out, I was directed to a box that asked me to verify that I was not a robot. This got me thinking about the strange competition we *real-life* realtors are now encountering since Zillow literally moved into our neighborhoods.

There's no doubt that our industry has become more and more automated. For example, at a click-of-a-button Zipform fills in by default, many of our negotiated / assumed time tables *without* us giving it much of a thought. Then, add to the equation people's desire for a tech-easy life, not to mention the ever-present debate that realtors get paid too much "for nothing", it's almost as though *real-life* realtors are becoming something of the past.

However, I am not the least bit worried about it.

Don't get me wrong. There's no doubt that products like Zipform and similar programs have made our life much easier as professionals. And, there's no question that Zillow *does* step on our earning potential toes. But in my 30 years in Real Estate, I've learned that at the end of the day, not every decision by a buyer or seller is made strictly on dollars and cents, or objective data alone. The truth of the matter is that the purchase of a home is still grounded in emotion. And last I checked, Siri cannot find that information in her database.

Meaning, she cannot convey why there is value in location. Or understand the history of a home. Or convey the subjective reason why a purchase might be a good fit, even if the comps don't substantiate it. Siri cannot tell your client which local team's coaches are the best. Or what growing old might feel like in the home of their dreams. Or where the Christmas tree will fit perfectly in the house.

In the day of robot competition, it is important to remember that not a single computer or software can create emotion or comprehend the needs of your clients.

But *you*, as a non-robot realtor, can. *You* can empathize with the needs of your client. *You* can find the creative ways to close the deal. *You* can seek and find the house with the exact nuances your special clients need.

But *you* (in the day of complacency), must make the commitment to click the box and not act like a robot. Instead, put your *real-life* human personality on and continue to perform like the passionate realtor you are, selling your clients the house of their dreams. Flaws and all, *real-life* realtors are still the best deal in town.

Reality Check:
Seek to understand your client's needs.

* * *

The Six Things to Remain a *Real-Life* Realtor, Not a Robot

- **COMPENSATION** – Though commission makes our human heart pound, it is important that you take that pulse out of the equation. Your sole focus is what's best for your client, and how can you accomplish that task. You must trust that the compensation will take care of itself, as long as you do your job.

- **BE THOUROUGH** – In the day and age of click and submit, your *real-life* element is to approach each aspect of the deal with thoroughness. Meaning don't rely on "autofill", but instead take the time to insert every date, data and detail of the offer yourself, to ensure that it accurately reflects every aspect of your client's intent and offers all the protection your client deserves.

- **NO AMBIGUITY** – As all programs have a back button for review, we *real-life* realtors must not be embarrassed of redundancies. It is better to confirm a contingency removal, or an inclusion of a personal property, or an inspection aspect more than once, rather than not at all.

- **VALUATION** – The number one value-for-money that we agents have over computers is that we can look, evaluate and feel the needs of our clients and their properties. Therefore, look for the intangible aspects of the property and merge that with your client's perception of value.

- **HONESTY** – A computer can perhaps list a fact. But a *real-life* realtor is able to provide an honest opinion. When it comes to deficiencies of a potential listing, don't be shy. An accurate list price can make all the difference between a sale versus an expired listing, and in the trust between you and your client.

- **RELATIONSHIP** – At the end of the day, people want to do business with people. Nothing replaces a strong hand shake and an eye-to-eye dialogue. The human element, or the real-life Realtor will never go out of fashion. No matter how quickly technology advances.

Sold – Represented Seller

Location:	Laguna Beach, California
Value 2021:	$7,100,000
Lot Size:	34,412 sqft
House Size:	4,000 sqft
Bedrooms:	4
Bathrooms:	4
Garage:	2 car

Almost a flat full acre in a private gated beach community.

Chapter 17

RISING ABOVE THE "HOBBYISTS"

Raising the Bar because it's Not Monkey Business

I recently met yet another person who made a statement that has never sat well with me. It was, "Oh, I dabble in real estate as well." Their nonchalant attitude about an industry I love, rubbed against my professional pride. Why? Because somehow they made it "acceptable" that my 30-something years of being a student in, and leader of the Real Estate industry, put us on the same playing field of expertise, merely because we held the same license.

It's a pity our industry responsibilities are taken so nonchalantly and that all agents consider themselves "equals" based off of holding the same credentials. Clients are trusting us with their most important asset, and yet somehow it is "okay" for anyone to hold the position who can pass a test – which is easier to pass than a cosmetology license exam.

Reality Check:
Don't deal with dabblers or hobbyists.

If you doubt the validity of what I'm saying, think about this: We would never go to a doctor with our important health issues who "dabbles" in medicine; nor would we hand-over our pressing legal issues to a lawyer, whose primary income stream was yoga instructing.

Don't get me wrong. I'm a champion of new agents entering our profession, as well as part-timers who are raising their families, or making a career move. As long as they have an authentic soul, meet or strive to exceed fiduciary duties, and take the steps to evolve and stay current on the latest trends with education that is necessary to be at the top of their game, I welcome them with open arms. But as the outspoken critic on raising the state of our profession, we need "buyer beware" warnings that differentiate the seasoned agent from the Hobbyist.

Some might scoff at my opinion but consider this. Webster's dictionary defines a Hobbyist as: (n.) a person who regularly or occasionally engages in an activity as a pastime rather than as a profession. Its synonyms are dabbler, amateur, layman, nonexpert, nonprofessional, or my favorite, a tinkerer. Unlike other industries, our profession is saturated with the Hobbyist.

Think how often you see a substantial listing with an inexperienced agent who turns out to be a brother, sister or relative of the seller? Or, though I love to mentor, think about how much time you "donate" to educating the Hobbyist on protocols, or how to keep the deal alive, only to see the advice is not always well received.

The question then becomes, "How did the bar for entry into our profession become so low, and the rate for failure so very high?"

It's Not Monkey Business

There is an unrealistic expectation that claims that once someone passes the real estate exam, all that's required to close a deal is to put the property in the MLS, place a sign out front, and sit back and wait for the money to flow. Well, that my friend is a task an evolved monkey can do. As I have said before, this business is much more than that.

The truth of the matter is that with the ever-emerging competition and online entities, we as "Blood, Sweat and Tears" Realtors, or as my PR Agent Paula Steurer (Sterling Public Relations) says, "Those with skin in the game", have to stay on top by ever-evolving, and making sure our primary goal is to protect the wellbeing of our client and their asset or investment. In other words, as a non-hobbyist, we need to constantly work on the things that set us apart from the Hobbyist.

So how does one make the transition from a Hobbyist Realtor, to a respected and evolved Realtor, who is worthy of every dollar earned of the commission associated with the deal? I have a "Raise the Bar", Six-Step Guideline:

1. Know Your Product: This means not being the evolved monkey, but instead to know every property in your area that is listed, every property that is in escrow, and every property that has sold; as well as understand the valuation behind each transaction.

2. Invest in your Marketing: In other words, be prepared to invest in your brand. That means making sure your Social Media presence and other marketing pieces are clean, concise, and up to date.

3. Manage your Clients Expectations: This means that at all times, to be prepared to tell your clients the truth in all aspects of the transaction. You might lose a few listings in the short run, but this one integrity move will set yourself apart from those that give inflated values just to get the listing and waste valuable market time.

4. Know Your Industry: This means never placing your client in a compromising position because you did not pay attention to every detail in the contract. This means knowing the RPA (Residential Purchase Agreement) inside and out. This means making sure every disclosure that you and your client is offering is filled out with the utmost care and detail, so that your file has strength and traction for all possible scrutiny.

5. Know Your Place: This means always remembering that you are a Realtor. Meaning, you are not an attorney, nor are you a contractor. So, play within the lines of your professionalism and keep your advice limited to your role as a Realtor. If you are doing your job professionally, that within itself will be more than enough to keep you engaged and busy for the duration of the transaction.

6. Most important, Know Your "Why." This means, knowing why you became a Realtor. In other words, it means knowing why you have chosen to be the" Real Deal", versus a Hobbyist. This means having not just skin in the game, but as I like to say, it means having "S.O.U .L. in the game" where beyond the commission, as a professional Realtor, you take that 1am call when your client is anxious about their life's investment and needs assurance that their dream house is possible. Or most importantly, it means being a facilitating dream-maker, who goes that extra mile because you genuinely care about the deal, about the client, and most obvious as a non-Hobbyist, you care about the memories you create for real-life human beings, who have real-life dreams. And you do it, because you are a proud, licensed, professional, Realtor.

So, don't just raise the bar on yourself and on our profession but instead be the bar that others will aspire to.

Sold – Represented Buyer/Seller

Location:	Newport Beach, California
Value 2021:	$6,800,000
Lot Size:	3,778 sqft
House Size:	3,778 sqft
Bedrooms:	5
Bathrooms:	5
Garage:	2 car

Property features a 55 ft dock and 2 side ties. I loved doing open houses there as for obvious reasons. I was also able to commute to the house with my boat.

Chapter 18

CHECK YOUR BANK ACCOUNT BEFORE YOU COMMIT!

(6 Ways to Service What You Wish For)

WHEN I was in college, I dated a very well-known and desired socialite. I was crazy for this beautiful woman. When she accepted a first date, I was over the moon! When she accepted a second date, I was happy. When she accepted a third date, I suddenly understood the saying, "Be careful what you wish for."

My life lesson happened somewhere between the moment my 24-year-old good looks and charm ran into the reality of my manorexic wallet. Within three dinner dates, my entire annual dating budget was blown. And with it, the short-lived romance had ended in mutual disappointment.

I share this story because I see the same dynamic in the world of real estate. The "dream-listing-of-the-day" client finally calls us, and before we think it through, we jump into the deal without being fully prepared to assess, understand, and execute the special needs of a luxury property.

As an advocate for encouraging agents to always "up their sight line" in real estate, the question then becomes, "How do you make the transition from a one million-dollar listing agent to the golden egg, 10-million plus-dollar luxury market?" Or, in other words, how do you know when you have the money in your wallet to date and keep the girl? The answer is:

Reality Check:
Make sure you have your big kid pants on when taking on a luxury listing.

If you are interested in learning how to make the "jump into the luxury" market when the beautiful girl comes knocking, below are six steps to success to effectively market a luxury property.

Six Steps to Success to Effectively Market a Luxury Property:

1. **Be clear on what a luxury listing is. (aka, know who you are dating):**
   The first step into the luxury market requires you to understand the term "luxury market." That said, the rule of thumb is that the luxury market is identified as "The top 10% of sales in that market." For the sake of explanation, let me use my area of Newport Beach as an example. In our area, the top 10 percent of the sales (i.e., the luxury market) starts at five million dollars plus. This means that 90% of the sales are below five million, and our luxury threshold starts at $6,200,000. As there is not a set dollar amount that identifies the "luxury market" and prices for "luxury listing" varies per area, your job as a newbie in the luxury world is to know your luxury market price point in your area.

2. **Have capital. (aka, check your bank account before you choose the restaurant):**
   When it comes to dining, you would never serve a 5-star dinner with plastic forks and knives. In the luxury market, you never offer a low-end marketing campaign to your high-end clients. The bottom line is that a brochure and marketing campaign for a $15,000,000 listing will be vastly different than a brochure for a $500,000 listing. For example, my recent oceanfront listing ($16,000,000) features a

16-page brochure alongside a video and drone footage that tells a lifestyle story. In addition, we have magazine placements, website visibility, digital placements and even events that create a buzz for the Who's Who in that area. Why do this? Because your high-end clients expect it.

3. **Look the part. (aka, dress properly for the date, so she knows you are a future someone, not a future cellmate):**
When you have a luxury property listing, you must look the part. You must be well-dressed and display an attitude of confidence and professionalism. The buyers and agents that preview listings are not first-time buyers or new agents. They are sophisticated buyers with sharp and savvy agents that have been around the block a few times …especially the luxury block. Your client, therefore, needs to know you are up to the task to best represent both them and the luxury property they are selling.

4. **Know your product. (aka, know your manners and which fork is used for what food):**
As a luxury agent, it is imperative to be entrenched in the intricacies of the luxury market. For example, in Newport Coast, the location of a home that is separated by one lot could mean a difference of $3,000,000 for the same lot size and the same type of home. Why is that? The reason is because, at night, one lot looks at the lit harbor and the other looks at black ocean. The moral of the story is that when it is time to make a price adjustment, you will need to present your client with real-time market information on their product.

5. **Have grit. (aka, be the gentleman for the duration of the relationship, not just for the first few dates):**
Grit is defined as passion and perseverance for the long-term goal. When dealing with luxury properties, the market time can often exceed 400 days. Therefore, before you say "yes" to the listing, you must ask yourself two questions:

A) Are you prepared to invest what it takes for that projected period and beyond?

B) Do you have the capital and ability to carry this listing for an extended period?

If you answer "No" to the two questions above, the problem is this: You have now utilized your entire annual marketing budget on a property that failed to meet your and your client's expectations with no ROI (return on investment) to show for it.

6. **Be discerning with your abilities and the client's expectations. (aka, know when she is just out of your league):**

    I know it can be very tempting to take a trophy listing, but before you say "Yes," make sure you accept the listing on terms you CAN deliver, but also go beyond the client's expectation. My favorite saying is, "I want to be the firstborn, second husband, and third listing agent because at that point the client will be much more realistic when it comes to actual market value."

If you read the above and say, "Wow, unfortunately, that's not me!" I don't want you to get discouraged. The good news is that there is an opportunity for you to go to the next level in your real estate career. For example, you can refer the listing and get a 25% referral fee. Better yet, you can partner with someone in your office who is already selling luxury listings. The exposure and educational curve will create a win-win for both you and your client, as the partnership will keep you in the deal and, most importantly, your client will get the representation he or she deserves. Best of all, if everyone does their job well, the success of the transaction will make it possible for you to not only get to the third date, but maybe even gain a client for life who will be speaking your praise to others. That, in turn, will result in more luxury referrals to you.

May the luxury market be a place of growth, comfort, and prosperity to you!

Sold – Represented Buyer/Seller

Location:	Newport Coast, California
Value 2021:	$5,500,000
Lot Size:	10,508 sqft
House Size:	4,300 sqft
Bedrooms:	5
Bathrooms:	5
Garage:	3 car

Property features a commercial rock pool with waterfalls, slide and grotto that you would find in a resort.

Chapter 19

STOP PLAYING MUSICAL CHAIRS...

It's Not Them, it's YOU

8 Important Questions You Need to Ask Prior to Backing-Up The Moving Van

It's time to be vulnerable and shine a little light on my past behavior. I'm prompted to do this to illustrate a point very dear to my heart, as it relates to both personal and professional growth.

At the age of 60, I came to the realization that I am a Narcissist. I'm sure that is no drum roll to some, but to me it was a huge insight to my behavior.

The good news is that today with lots of personal work, I consider myself a "Narcissist in Recovery"; which in general terms means that, rather than offend 90% of the people I come in contact, I only offend 40% of those I encounter.

For those not familiar with Narcissism, one thing we are *really* good at is, blaming everyone else for things that go wrong. Or more candidly stated, we get "mad", disappointed in others, or throw adult temper-tantrums if what we "expect", doesn't come in the package we feel we deserve. Then, to make sure everyone knows we are unhappy, we throw the baby out with the bathwater by arrogantly blaming others for everything that is "wrong" and stomp out of the room (or leave a brokerage) determined to prove that the grass is greener, once the "idiots" in our life are behind us. In personal life, I call this immaturity. In business I call it, Musical Chairs.

> **Musical Chairs (n): "a situation in which people frequently exchange jobs of positions"**

In our industry, I see a lot of Musical Chair Realtors. Meaning I see agents who jump ship because they continue to find discontent with firm after firm. Or, agents who quickly change business cards because they are blinded by the "Bright and Shiny New Object" syndrome when new companies come to town and offer "pies in the skies" new technology, not yet implemented or proven to work or, a piece of the "rock" (that might just be a mere sand dune). Or agents who prefer to throw blame balls at the teams or companies they work with because their personal performance is lacking.

Don't misunderstand what I am saying. Speaking from firsthand experience I certainly understand the need to move brokerages on occasion. I am contemporary enough to know that the days of a person staying at one job or company for a lifetime is long gone. Certainly, it is the norm for any of us to make a few upward moves over a period of time as we ascend in our profession.

But that type of shift and movement is not what I'm talking about. Today I want to address what I call the Serial Musical Chair Realtor and help identify the difference between playing real estate musical chairs, versus creating authentic shift and change for career success.

A Serial Musical Chair Realtor is someone who moves from company to company, always looking for the greener grass. They are someone who eventually finds discontent in every firm they join and much like the Narcissist, will blame the destruction of their career on others rather than own the responsibility of their profession themselves.

It is no doubt that changing firms is a big decision. Our instability, or too much mobility not only dilutes our personal brand but causes a lack of confidence in our clients as well. Therefore, if you find yourself discontent (again) in your current firm, or are considering moving to a new brokerage, here are 8 questions to consider before you move.

Reality Check:
Don't be a musical chair realtor.

The 8 important questions before moving firms

1. Before moving companies, make sure you understand your WHY. Meaning, what needs do you currently have that are not getting met at your existing company?

2. Make sure before jumping ship you have clearly discussed these needs with your current broker. Or in other words, have you given your current company the opportunity to make changes? And if "yes", what is the timeline for these changes to be implemented?

3. If you choose to leave, make sure you have vetted your new company and ask yourself, is the new company aligned with your personal brand? Is it a company that you can become the best definition of Self?

4. Does your new company have a guarantee that the needs you are requesting will be executed? And what happens if they do not perform?

5. Before you jump, does this new company have the track record that proves they are a Rockstar, versus a karaoke singer? Meaning, will they be a group you just "work" for/with? Or will they become a family you can grow and expand with and more importantly a company that will be there for you when the market fluctuates? Are they interested in "You" as an agent/broker? Or are they just after your market share? Do they have the infrastructure to withstand the market changes? And do they have the capital committed to offer the on-going support required for sustainability even in a down market?

6. Is your decision to leave fear based or what's truly best for you and your future…fear-based decisions hardly ever work out for anyone. And is this move truly a better opportunity or a promise of things based on false assurances?

7. The things that are enticing you to leave, are they a short-term bandage or a long-term solution?

8. Finally, coming from a "Narcissist in Recovery" who spent years looking for the next best thing, make sure you examine your ego and ask yourself, is your change rooted in clarity and strategic movement, or is it your ego? An ego that is pouting because you didn't get your way, and now, you are taking your marbles elsewhere. An ego that keeps you on the never-ending game of being a Serial Musical Chair Realtor. An ego that is always looking for the next best thing rather than buckling down and appreciating what you have in your current firm.

At the end of the day we are responsible for our own professional and personal success. And when things don't go our way it is easy for us to throw blame balls at our team and tell ourselves the narrative that we are not content at our brokerage because "they" are the issue.

Maturity is learning that success and happiness is not found in every new shiny object that comes knocking at our door, but instead having the wisdom to see opportunities for what they really are…

If you find the time is right for you to make that move, make sure you do it with dignity and class and not like a thief in the night, and letting your boss know that you have moved on by walking into an empty office in the morning.

Remember, the grass is not always greener on the other side…most of the time it turns out to be AstroTurf. So, an important question before you jump is, where will you sit when the music stops playing…

Sold – Represented Buyer/Seller

Location: Corona Del Mar, California
Value 2021: $6,200,000
Lot Size: 5,520 sqft
House Size: 4,000 sqft
Bedrooms: 4
Bathrooms: 3
Garage: 2 car

Property features direct white-water views from every level.

Chapter 20

TALES FROM THE SANDBOX

5 Steps to Working Well with Other Agents

For many years I was on a self-centered journey where I thought all roads led back to Self. I honestly believed during that time that the "sandbox" I played or resided in, was either all mine; or at least, a "territory" governed by my rules and expectations.

I don't mention my personal issues to receive a badge of honor. Rather, I mention *them* because I'm seeing a prevalent behavior, or more like an ugly industry birthmark rising in our profession that I call the "Not Playing Nicely in the Sandbox" syndrome.

There's no doubt that from time-to-time we are all guilty of the "My Sandbox, My Rules" attitude. Meaning, we all want to believe that the road to a successful transaction runs through us. But just as selfishness is not the right ingredient for a flourishing personal life, it also doesn't transfer into our business life either. Successful transactions require us to work together as co-creators of the deal, so all parties win.

As one of the personalities on Bravo TV's "Real Estate Wars", I know the irony of that statement. We spent 8 pompous weeks showing-off our amazing properties and glamorizing the drama and problems of the deal.

But let's be clear. That was for television. As cast members, we had to create the "All About Me Deal", as viewers would never hold on for one more episode if the cliffhanger for the week included our going over the results of the termite inspection.

In our complex and competitive world of luxury real estate, business reality is much different. In the real-life world, it is imperative to not only be on top of your personal game, but equally so, to have a strong working relationship with fellow agents. Remember, our clients expect to get the best of both sides of the deal. Our job therefore, is to finesse our way through the offers and counter-offers to get it for them. Our job is to keep the negative emotions at bay, so communications remain open. Our job is to meet the expectations of both sides of the transaction, so the deal closes. The only way to make this happen is to have a strong working relationship with the other agent; which means, who you do business with on the other end, plays nicely in the sandbox, and you do as well.

So, what does "playing nicely in the sandbox" look like? National Association of Realtors (NAR) has spelled out our professional conduct in their "Code of Ethics", which can be found at `www.nar.realtor/about-nar/governing-documents/code-of-ethics/the-code-of-ethics`. However, for the layman reader, I have created my 5 Rules to the Sandbox, which are as follows:

Reality Check:
You must be an agent others want to work with.

The 5 Rules to Playing Nicely in the Sandbox

1. **Share Your Toys:** There is a saying I have always embraced, and that is, "You do not know what you do not know." Therefore if, and when an agent asks you for your professional opinion, give an intellectual donation to the industry and provide your knowledge. Many times, you might be the expert in your area and someone might need to draw upon your

years of experience to make a deal work. If you are called upon, share your wisdom, as someday you might need to call upon someone else for theirs.

2. Allow Others into Your Box: No transaction can take place in a vacuum with only you in the sandbox. In other words, you are not an island. You are hired by your clients not just for your ability to put a home in the MLS (as a monkey can do that); you are also hired for your marketing, negotiating and your ability to find the people who are in the market for their property, or who represent the type property they are looking to purchase. In other words, networking with other people is a must for success in our industry.

3. Don't Squawk in the Box: In our business, some agents feel that gossip is Gold or a form of currency. In an industry that deals with the spillage of divorce or financial ruin that puts houses on the market, there's no doubt that you will hear things from the other agents or clients that are as juicy as fat on a piece of steak. As a professional however, you must be aware of inflammatory communications. Negotiations can get emotional enough as they are. Your job is to be the filter that keeps the deal between the railings.

4. Be Polite & Courteous: In an industry that's saturated with part-timers (or *hobbyists*, as I have referred to them in a previous article), it's unavoidable to encounter an agent who is not on your level, or who are not as accomplished as you are. When you do encounter these agents, rather than get frustrated and speak to them like they are in kindergarten, remember you probably learned to climb the jungle gym years before them.

5. Keep the Sandbox Clean & Orderly: If you study the greatest leaders in the world, one of their common traits is "order." I mention that because the Rule of Order also applies to the sandbox. As a Realtor, one of your jobs is to keep your files accurate and orderly. This is especially important if, and when an issue arises after the Close of Escrow. But more so, this important discipline will allow you to focus on managing your client and the deal, all while maintaining accurate and orderly files for a successful closing. For all you, *non-paperwork types*, don't use your lack of enthusiasm for detail as an excuse. There are Transaction Coordinators available for hire who can maintain the detail work for you.

As authentic industry experts, let's continue to raise the bar of practice in our industry by this year committing to "Playing Nicely in the Sandbox." It will not only lead to less injuries in the transaction process, but more so, to create a win-win for all.

Sold – Represented Seller

Location:	Newport Coast, California
Value 2021:	$6,300,000
Lot Size:	13,187 sqft
House Size:	5,500 sqft
Bedrooms:	5
Bathrooms:	5
Garage:	4 car

Has a Chef's kitchen that rivals any professional kitchen.

Chapter 21

Arm Wrestling with Artificial Intelligence

3 Steps to becoming a Relevant Realtor in a Changing Market

I was reading an article the other day that led with, "Millions of workers around the world are at risk of losing their jobs to robots or A. I. (Artificial Intelligence), but it's Americans who should be particularly worried."

At first, I didn't pay much attention to the daunting statement because my area of expertise is Real Estate, not retail or production, and last I checked, my two metal hips haven't added a single contribution to the closing of any deal. However, as I dove deeper into the read, the threat of A.I. and job security peaked my curiosity when the article informed me that, "thirty-eight percent of jobs in the U.S. are a high risk of being replaced by robots and artificial intelligence," according to a new report by PwC.

I must confess, I have never thought of myself as a Rocket Scientist. That's why I never imagined that a robot or A.I. could take my place of selling homes in my local market. That is, until now. And here is why I've changed my opinion.

If you look at our industry through a traditional lens, our formula for success has been based on a threefold foundation. 1) The development of personal relationships. 2) The alignment with the right firm and a professional, branded image. 3) The occasional mano-a-mano "farming" turf war to prove we are the most qualified agent in the are*a*, *due* to the excessive saturation of realtors, in majority of zip codes.

So, how is it that A.I. could possibly infiltrate our human bubble? The answer is, it already has. Meet Zillow, Realestate.com, and Trulia: The Artificial Intelligent "Realtors" of the future.

Before you panic and move to an aluminum covered bunker, let me assure you that Real Estate A.I. replacement will not happen overnight. Life-like robots and in-home cameras that replace live showings are not yet here. But let's not be like my good friend and *uber* successful buddy *Steve, (named changed for the sake of long term friendship) who years ago told me not to waste my time with this thing called, "The Internet". He claimed it would never last. More than likely his comment was made, out of fear. Fear of change. Fear of the unknown. Fear of having to learn to embrace something new into our often "routine" lives.

Today, the reality for most industries is that A.I. *is* the wave of the future. Most people today will consider buying a home without an agent, but only a very small percentage of all closed transactions are completed without the services of a real estate agent.

Reality Check:
Clients will always need our patience, assurance and problem solving skills.

Technology is advancing at stunning rates, and giants like Zillow and other on-line entities are continuing to develop systems and programs that put them in direct competition with the services we offer our clients.

Add to it, that clients are learning to shop not just for homes, but for everything in new ways, and all signs point to the fact that if we don't pay attention to what is happening, we will soon be irrelevant Realtors. The question then becomes, how do we maintain being a *Relevant Realtor* in light of emerging A.I. giants? The answer is that we become a Relevant Realtor.

3 Steps to Remaining a Relevant Realtor

1. **Remember that A.I. or Zillow cannot Define Value:** My father, who was both an attorney and one of the smartest guys I've known, always told me "Son, a little bit of knowledge is very dangerous." His point was that disseminating or depending on information can be dangerous, when we rely on "it" to be the expert opinion.

As a *Relevant Realtor*, you must remember that though Zillow is a giant company, it by no means is an entity that can define value. By its own admission, Zillow stated in 2018 that their ZESTimates are right only 40% of the time. And by "right", they mean properties selling within 5% of their ZEST-imate. This means that 60% of the time, their ZEST-imate is wrong. (Zillow 2015)

As we all know, properties and their respective valuations are not solely driven by data. Therefore, as a *Relevant Realtor*, you have an advantage that A.I. does not, which is articulating the subjective and objective value and assessment of properties.

Score Card: Human Realtor: 1. A.I.: 0

2. **Remember that Alexa Cannot Hold your Clients Hand:** Buying or selling a home is never a nerve-less process. As we've all experienced, clients come in many packages with various personalities and visions for their ideal property. Some buyers want a home on the water. Some want

a home in the woods. Some care more about the bottom line of the deal. Others want to know how the roses in the yard were planted. All however have one thing in common- they all are putting their earnings and dreams within the transaction we are helping navigate.

As a *Relevant Realtor*, no matter how advanced technology becomes, clients will always need a human hand to hold through the stressful process. Meaning, clients will always need our calming guidance and advice when the world of mortgage or inspections becomes overwhelming. They will always need our hawk eye of protection over all points of the deal. They will always need our patience and assurance if the deal goes into a stall. And they will especially need our caring and comfort if the deal falls out of escrow and they see their dreams crash with it.

The reality of our industry is that no matter how much technology advances, human buyers and sellers still need a human Realtor; as last time I checked, asking Alexa for comfort before the close of the deal is no less soothing than shaking a Magic 8 Ball to see how your kids will end up in life. It still takes a Hands-on-Realtor, not A.I. robots and systems, to calm a buyer's nerves.

Score Card: Human Realtor: 2. A.I.: 0

3. Remember that Siri is Not Always Available, and she has No Moral Code: I recently bought myself a new car. I was in route to an important meeting and needed Siri to provide me with a quick piece of information. I pushed her button, stated my request, and in turn she flashed her iridescent "thinking" line, then disingenuously said, "I'm sorry. Something seems to be wrong. I cannot help you with that right now." And with that, our conversation was over.

Ah, yet another *Relevant Realtor* advantage - The ability to be available to our clients. This means being available with your time, available with your information, available with industry facts, available with answers, and most importantly, available with something that Artificial Intelligence can never provide, which is an Integrity Code of Conduct that does, in fact, care about the needs of your client.

Final Score: Human Realtor: 3. A.I.: 0

As our industry heads towards a technology-based future, I do highly recommend staying current on all the latest trends. However, to maintain your relevance as a professional realtor in your area, remember we are not in an arm wrestling match with A.I. Instead, online services are here to provide us with extended tools to simplify our lives and expand our awareness. Today, Relevant Realtors remember that at the end of the day, the winning move happens when we show *up as* the best human version of ourselves; then do what we know how to do best, which is to service our clients, both professionally and personally with soul.

Sold – Represented Seller

Location: Laguna Beach, California
Value 2021: $5,400,000
Lot Size: 4,791 sqft
House Size: 2,400 sqft
Bedrooms: 3
Bathrooms: 2
Garage: 3 car

Has a saltwater pool with 180-degree ocean view. Owner did a complete Hawaiian makeover.

Chapter 22

FACE-OFF: ON WHAT SIDE OF THE DESK DO YOU SIT?

The 7 Don'ts of Great Leadership

THE other day I had an extremely complex and convoluted transaction. I was getting so focused on closing the deal that I started to lose sight of the solution. Like any smart agent, I sought the second opinion of my Brokers. As I sat across the desk from their wealth of knowledge, I quickly remembered the importance of great leadership. After ten minutes under their sound counsel, I had a fresh perspective and solution to my problem.

The desk-side encounter got me thinking about the importance of leadership in our industry. Though many would say that the days of traditional brokerages are quickly fading, I happen to disagree. I still believe there is a place and need for a traditional brokerage firm in our industry, that not only leads by mentorship, but more so, by example. The three-fold question then becomes, "What does great leadership look like? What does it not look like?" And, "Is there room at the table to sit on both sides of the desk?"

Before I continue, I want to let you know that the firm I chose to hang my broker's license under now, is only my second brokerage firm in my

30 plus years in the industry. Obviously, I don't make a habit of playing musical chairs with my brokerages, but the combination of my years in real estate, as well as, having served as the President of our association there is one thing for sure, I have experienced the difference between good leadership and bad leadership.

Reality Check:
Great leadership does not divide its attention.

Having had the privilege of working under great leadership for the past 11 years I want to first outline the DO's of great leadership. That list includes:

- Provides accessibility by the leadership to the entire team.

- Creates a cooperative culture amongst its agents with information flowing freely, working as a team and not as individuals.

- Offers layers of support in all aspects of our business including weekly workshops, meetings and trainings on new technology.

- Operates with total transparency, and the compensation structure is known to all with no secret dealings.

- Is 100% dedicated to its agents and their quest for market share and long-term success.

- It is constantly evolving its image, brand, resources, training programs, and technology.

- It honors fiduciary duties to its agents by never forgetting that they are the Cornerstones of the company.

In addition to this list of leadership excellence, there is another and more important list that in my career history, I have never witnessed authentic leaders do. I call this list the *7 Don'ts of Great Leadership*.

The 7 Don'ts of Great Leadership

#1: Great leadership does not compete with their agents: Meaning, to be an effective leader or manager, you cannot be in direct or indirect competition with your agents to list or sell. In most areas, the ratio of clients-to-Realtors is such that many agents are competing for business from the same small client pool. You cannot sit on both seats and expect to have your agent's best interest at heart.

#2: Great Leadership does not divide its attention: As a leader, your focus must be your agents. Being both a Manager and an Agent is like being a cop and firefighter at the same time. Both are fulltime jobs.

Think about this logically. If a manager is showing their listings, taking buyers out to see property, holding broker previews, open houses, navigating escrows, and interfacing with their own clients, how much time is left to provide support to agents? And where is their attention being focused, on you and your clients, or on their own business and their clients?

At best, a manager who also operates as an agent, has a divided interest. At minimum they will have limited time for their fellow agents. At maximum, they will end-up in competition against their fellow agents for potential clients. Neither, is what I consider a win-win.

#3: Great Leadership does not offer secret deals as a recruiting or retention method: One of the biggest mistakes a firm can make is a lack of transparency. Too often, I have seen companies offer secret deals as an incentive to retain agents or attract agents to join their brokerage. Newsflash: These deals never stay secret and sooner than later other agents find out that they are not special anymore, and some new Hot Shot got a better deal. When these secret deals are discovered it causes dissention in the company. Plus, it is a non-sustainable formula.

I'm reminded of a friend who planned on joining our brokerage long before he finally did. But every time he talked about leaving his brokerage, the company kept throwing money at him to stay. The gimmick worked for a while, but as the company did not have the support, culture, and many other factors they needed to grow his business, the agent eventually left.

Please don't misunderstand, I totally endorse multiple levels of compensation/split based on performance, as long it is consistent and transparent to all.

#4: Great Leadership does not create a business model with the emphasis on selling the company: It used to be that selling a successful brokerage was a by-product of having built a successful company with substantial market share. Now-a-days, brokerages launch their companies with the premise of building a company that can be sold to a national chain within 5 or 10 years.

#5: Great Leadership does not make A.I. or technology their Cornerstone: A.I. and technology are very important components in a growing a successful brokerage, but they are secondary to hands-on management and daily human interaction.

#6: Great Leadership does not foster an attitude of individuals or lone rangers: You will never realize your potential or find success if you are working as an individual where the flow of information is not part of your daily routine. If there is a disconnect between you and your brokerage, there will be an inherent disconnect between you, and client retention.

#7: Great Leadership does not dishonor their fiduciary duties to their agents: Personally, I would like to be the boss of *everything*. However, as professionals we have a fiduciary duty when it comes to the roles we play. What I am saying is that, the ethical decision between "can" we sit in both seats, OR "should" we sit in both seats, needs to be addressed. I am reminded of a quote from the movie "Jurassic Park", that said: "Your scientists were so preoccupied with whether they could, they didn't stop to think if they should." That same question is what I am posing to our industry… "just because we can… should we?"

At the end of the day, Leadership is Leadership, and a true leader knows in which chair they should sit.

Sold – Represented Seller

Location:	Newport Coast, California
Value 2021:	$4,600,000
Lot Size:	10,500 sqft
House Size:	3,800 sqft
Bedrooms:	3
Bathrooms:	3
Garage:	3 car

This is a former model by the builder with a 270-degree view.

Chapter 23

Honey Badger Don't Care

The 4 Steps to Being Fearless

ONE day, a dear friend of mine who is a successful sales-driven business man, saw I was having one of those frustrating mornings where not one, but three deals appeared to be going sideways.

Sensing my pending frustration, my buddy looked at me with confident, yet humored eyes and said, "Come on Spee… Honey Badger Don't Care." It proved to be one of the best pieces of business advice I'd received in a long time.

If you are not familiar with a Honey Badger, a Honey Badger is a wild, four-legged animal that is a cross between the cartoon character Pepe Le Pew, and a miniature version of Baloo from The Jungle Book. His midget size legs and white skunk back make him look almost domesticated enough for the next family photo. However, don't let the 20 pounds of black and white cuddliness fool you. Honey Badger is one of the biggest bad-asses in the animal kingdom who fears almost nothing. For instance, if a Honey Badger wants Honey, despite of 1000 bee stings, he goes for the honey. Why? Because "Honey Badger Don't Care." If Honey Badger wants a snake? Despite of the venomous bites, he goes for the snake. Why? Because "Honey Badger Don't Care." When it comes to the grit, focus and staying power required to survive the wild, a Honey Badger's attitude to the challenges he faces is simply, "Honey Badger Just Don't Care!"

I share my newly found appreciation (and mantra) of "Honey Badger Don't Care" because too often I see agents become paralyzed with fear in the face of adversity. They fear rejection, solicitation, success, and they fear the deal going sideways. They fear not finding the next client, negotiations and contracts, the economy shifting, and they fear not being the "best *parent on the block*" because they are out fearfully chasing the next deal.

In my 30 plus years of real estate sales, one thing my Honey Badger mentality has taught me, is that if we are going to succeed in the world of sales and commission, we need to find our inner Honey Badger and live by the motto that says, "Honey Badger Don't Care."

Reality Check:
Be fearless and relentless in your pursuit of excellence.

The 4 Steps to Being Fearless and Finding Your Inner Honey Badger

1. **Identify Your Market:** Developing your inner Honey Badger takes awareness of where you eat. Meaning, to be successful at sales, we must eat, breathe and sleep our markets. This means knowing the nuances about every neighborhood, every street and every aspect of the lifestyle your market has to offer. The knowledge about every new listing, every pending sale, every closed sale, and every pocket listing will add to your confidence to go after what you know.

2. **Be Determined:** When Honey Badger wants Honey, he never lets a few thousand bees stop him. Therefore, when it comes to a saturated,

heavy Realty market, never be afraid to take on larger-than-life challenges. Just because there are agents in your area that have been there for years, does not mean you can't break into that market, as well.

3. Be Outcome Driven: When it comes to sustainability, Honey Badger doesn't let a little snake bite deter him either. If Honey Badger has committed to something, he will; despite of temporary pain, keep focused on his job. As a sustainable Realtor, you too must Not allow yourself to get side-tracked when the snake bites in life, penetrate your morals. The sting is only temporary, and if you stay focused, you can reboot to success.

4. Be a Risk Taker: One thing Honey Badger does not do, is back down. Be it from a little bee, or a giant buffalo, "Honey Badger Don't Care" about size. Therefore, when it comes to buying or selling real estate, we too need to have that fearless attitude as well. It is just as easy to sell a $10,000,000 home as it is to sell a $500,000 home. Success is not found in the number of deals you close, but more so, in the knowledge that your clients have a Honey Badger, as a realtor.

So, the next time you feel frustrated with clients, agent or deals find your inner Honey Badger and press on, because Honey Badgers just don't care!

Sold – Represented Seller

Location:	Newport Beach, California
Value 2021:	$4,700,000
Lot Size:	8,600 sqft
House Size:	5,130 sqft
Bedrooms:	4
Bathrooms:	4
Garage:	3 car

This property was also owned by my clients who owned one of the largest grocery company chains in California, (the importance of servicing your clients with the utmost care as there is a great deal of repeat business in every deal.)

Chapter 24

GREATNESS REQUIRES FEARLESS OBSESSION

(The 8 Steps to Creating Commitment)

PERHAPS you have been the target of a stalker. Or maybe you have been a stalker at one point in your life. Either way, the role of a stalker is to know every detail about his or her subject - even down to the smallest detail. As strange as it may sound, this is how we need to approach our commitment to our profession. Please allow me to explain:

In high school, I was a State wrestling champion and a National AAU champion. I didn't accomplish this because I treated my sport as a hobby. I accomplished this because I was obsessed with success. For instance, when most wrestlers in the mid 70's wrestled November through March, I wrestled all year long. I even wrestled during football season (which I also played), and even during the summer when most of my friends could be found at Corona Del Mar's Lifeguard Tower #5. I attended national training camps and wrestled guys much older and more experienced than me. I wrestled in the off-season, and I studied every aspect of the sport. By the time I graduated high school, I was the best in my class and I knew it. The reason for my success was because I had a "stalker" mentality.

Then came my hard life lesson. Fast forward to my freshman year in college where, due to my stalker mentality, I earned a full wrestling scholarship to UCLA. Unfortunately, in my first year, I not only cost the school more money than I was worth, but I found myself losing more matches than I won.

If you're curious about what happened, besides multiple surgeries and a bent ego, I stopped being obsessed about my sport. Maybe it was the distraction of a new girlfriend. Maybe it was my life at the Beta fraternity house. Or maybe more truthfully speaking, it was because I lost my commitment. When the going got tough and I didn't win every match I entered, I became a hobbyist or a dabbler in the sport. The end result was that I let my sport and school down, and most importantly, myself.

If you have followed my writings, you have probably noted that when it comes to the hobbyists in our profession, I am not a fan. Perhaps my wrestling lesson explains my conviction. I believe that, like wrestling, we can't just treat our profession as a hobby or a part-time job. We can't quit on our clients when a property does not sell in the first few months. We can't be frugal when it comes to marketing our properties. And we can't be uninformed about the constant fluctuations in our market. When it comes to our clients and our profession, we need to be fearless and obsessive.

Reality Check:
If you want to be the best, you must be obsessed.

In California, there are approximately 200,000 real estate agents. However, less than 20% make money in this profession. The question then becomes, what can we do to make sure we are not only in the 20% of agents who make a good living in real estate, but more so, be in the top 5% of agents who make a great living doing what they love? The answer is found in, what I call, "The 8 Steps to Creating Commitment."

The 8 Steps to Creating Commitment:

1. **Be Obsessed with Education:**
   Education is key when we face a market that keeps changing or find online entities that attempt to replace us. The rule of thumb, when it comes to staying on top of your game, is "Information in means information out." Therefore, to get into the top 5% of agents who make a great living doing what they love, is to stay educated. Education keeps you relevant and gives you the ability to answer complex questions and offer solutions to complex challenges.

2. **Be Obsessed with Passion:**
   If you are going to get into the top 5% of agents who make a great living doing what they love, you must be fueled by passion. Passion, during good times and rough times, is what will keep your engine running to stay in the business for the long haul.

3. **Be Obsessed with Success:**
   As a top 5% realtor, you must be clear on what success means to you. For me, it means not only making sure my clients' desired outcome is achieved, but I want to be able to exceed their expectations as well.

4. **Be Obsessed with Ethics:**
   In a world where the line often gets blurred when it comes to morality and ethics, leaders in our industry are those who operate their business beyond reproach. To me, ethics is knowing right from wrong and doubling down on right. Meaning, you never compromise on the "grey" area of your fiduciary obligations. You always put your client's interest ahead of yours.

5. **Be Obsessed with Perseverance:**
   If you start something, whether it is a new listing, a new branding campaign, or a new "farming" campaign, make sure you have two commitments under your business legs:
   A) Commit to finishing what you set out to do.
   B) Make sure you aspire to do it better than anyone else.

Let me use the example of "farming." Farming can come in the traditional geographical form or within your social sphere of influence. No matter which form it takes, though, be sure you are in it for the long haul. Don't send out two flyers and expect call backs. Farming is a year-long process that should be done every two weeks for the first 6 months and then monthly after that, if you want to make a real impact.

6. **Be Obsessed with being Compassionate:**
To be compassionately committed, your clients must know that you are not just selling an asset or commodity. This means your job as an agent is to be mindful of your client's family dynamics, their needs, and most important the "why" behind the transaction. Always remember, for you, it is a commission. For your client, it is potentially a lifetime decision.

7. **Be Obsessed with Reaching the Top:**
Our profession is not a low-hanging fruit that you pick out of default, but one that requires a ladder to climb to pick the best from the top branch.

8. **Be Obsessed with becoming the Best Version of Yourself:**
The best version of you is when all of the above are met, and you have created something that gives you purpose and identity.

To make it into the 5% of agents who are making a great living and reaping the rewards and the lifestyle that our industry can provide, you must be an agent with an obsession. You must be a realtor who resembles me when I was a young man obsessed with wrestling success. I went to bed every night thinking how I could do things better, and then I got up and did it better.

My questions to you are, "What percentile are you in, and are you obsessed enough to be the be the best?"

Sold – Represented Buyer/Seller

Location:	Newport Beach, California
Value 2021:	$4,500,000
Lot Size:	10,900 sqft
House Size:	5,288 sqft
Bedrooms:	4
Bathrooms:	5
Garage:	2 car

This property is in the most desirable guard gated golf community in Newport Beach.

Chapter 25

CHOOSING MINI-ME

(4 Elements to Finding the Right Protégé for the Sustainability Of Your Business)

ONE of my favorite movies of all time is the Austin Powers series. I love all the characters including Fat Bastard, Dr. Evil, and of course my favorite character was Mini-Me, the protégé of Dr. Evil.

Allow me to clarify that the use of the term Mini-Me in this article is not to infer that we, like the ego driven Dr. Evil, are to find a direct replica of self to sustain our business. Instead, my reference is to make the point that one element in building a sustainable real estate practice is finding a protégé that can help you maintain your business today, and more important, sustain your business in the future. In fact now more than ever in our business do I believe that we too must incorporate the mentor-protégé sustainability formula, to both keep an avenue of revenue streaming for our future, as well bring up young professionals whose contemporary strengths will position them to make a footprint of their own, the heels of a well-established business.

This topic is important to our industry because for the most part, realtors don't have official retirement dates. Meaning we don't show up to work one morning and have a stupid cake and maybe a Timex watch waiting for us for all our years of service. Reality is that as the years go on, we fade away and eventually stop doing deals because we are no longer relevant or contemporary enough to compete in this ever-changing and challenging market.

It's no doubt that the concept of finding a "Mini Me"" is not new to the business world. For example, young doctors who serve under seasoned doctors take over well-established practices all in good time. Parents pass on to their children established companies once they have proven their ability to successfully manage and grow the business. For our industry though, the importance of "protégé building" is not widely discussed.

This gap in information exists probably because most young and hungry agents are not necessarily eager to sit in the student seat. Most want to be their own boss, to have their name on the proverbial door, and to make the bigger split of the commission and not be accountable to anyone. I believe part of the reason is that the perception of what we do seems easy and effortless when the truth couldn't be more opposite.

The question then becomes, in a day and age when the competition is tough and egos run high, *how* do you find the right Mini Me?"

In my previous chapter called "The 7 C's of group success", I addressed the basic elements of mentoring. This time therefore, I want to step deeper into the subject by giving you some protégé principles that can lead to long term partnerships, with the goal of being that when you are ready to step into your retirement, you will still have residual income from your clientele that now is entrusted into your capable hands of your protégé.

As I reflect on this subject, I am reminded of a very successful real estate team within the Surterre brand that started working together in 2010. They are one of the top producers in the Laguna Beach (OC) Luxury market, and to this day, the team is still working together in a reduced capacity; even after the senior member moved away and only comes to town for a few selected deals.

Their names are Michael Gosselin and Frank Hufnagel. Their brief history is that Michael took Frank under his wing in 2010 as a mentor, and Frank in return was an incredible asset to the team as an ambitious mentee. As the years passed, the compensation and responsibilities eventually shifted, to where Frank became the primary force behind the team and Michael was able to move away yet still receive benefits from the group. This success story is a perfect example creating sustainability, as it shows that with the right formula everyone wins. So, what is that winning formula? They contain four elements.

Having had both unsuccessful and successful proteges over the past 30 plus years here is what I have discovered are 4 important elements to building sustainability.

1. Begin by finding a more contemporary/younger protégé who you are willing to take a risk with, and just like Mini-Me, DO make sure they are very similar to you.

If both of you are similar in age, it defeats the purpose of being able to take a step back and focus on more personal goals. Your protégé should be at least 10 to 15 years younger in order to continue the business and relationships you have developed and take them to the next level. Your clients might be getting older as well, but they still want to have it all…A relationship with you that they trust and can depend on and the knowledge of you being contemporary enough to handle the ever-changing market and that is where your protégé comes in.

As much as you need to embrace some important differences in the two of you such as the approach to technology, social media and marketing it is paramount that your core values are aligned and your approach to what has made you successful remains the primary focus.

2. Once you find that Mini-Me, make sure they bring attributes and qualities to the table that are different than you.

I have found over the years that I don't know what I don't know…meaning that I get very set in my way of doing business that I don't look for new and improved ways of servicing my clients. That is where your protégé can lead you into being the best version of yourself that you can be.

3. Create an environment that fosters loyalty on both sides as *your* clients will eventually become your *joint* clients; and finally, his or her clients.

Trust and loyalties are not only earned but take time. It will take time for you to trust that this is not a quick stop over for your protégé but a long-term commitment that will eventually lead to you and your protégé being interchangeable in your client's eyes.

At the same time your protégé must feel that you are 100% committed to this partnership and are vested to the point that they are empowered to do the tasks that will lead them eventually to being recognized as an equal.

The fruit of this "give and take" is that one day their name will be added to the proverbial door (group name) and eventually your name will be removed as it becomes their journey now, with residual income still coming your way.

4. Define early if this is an internship or a potential future partnership

If it is an internship, have a beginning and an end date and don't get too attached. Give the best you have to offer to the intern and utilize their quest for experience for your daily tasks. If it is a relationship that will grow into a partnership, be prepared to put your ego aside and be a mentor. Encourage your protégé to swim in the deep end of the pool instead of the shallow end where they may have been hanging out in prior to meeting you.

The value that you have and will continue to deposit into your Mini-Me will all be returned to you by keeping you sustainable when it comes to evolving your brand into a market that is constantly changing in terms of technology, automation and the ever-growing social media presence.

I love what I do, and I hope to be doing this for many more years to come, as doing deals is in my blood and gives me a reason to get up in the morning. However, eventually my time at the Moana Surfrider in Honolulu or at our place in Greece will become more extended and I need to make sure that I have a Mini-Me in place that will not only allow me to remain vital and involved but will also cover me when I am away.

So, let's choose wisely when it comes to whom you let into our "house" …I hope you will all find your "Mini-Me" in your pursuit of future relevance.

Sold – Represented Buyer

Location:	Newport Beach, California
Value 2021:	$4,300,000
Lot Size:	9,435 sqft acres
House Size:	4,510 sqft
Bedrooms:	5
Bathrooms:	5
Garage:	3 car

This client is one of my favorite clients and she has the Midas Touch. Single mom, two amazing boys and everything she touches turns to gold. She makes my job very enjoyable and exciting. Her Superbowl parties are legendary and this back yard certainly helps in that.

Chapter 26

The "Who" Behind the Public "You"

(Great Agents Remember the "WHO")

Open any page on any social media platform and it is easy to see that we live in an ego-focused culture where social media is all about "YOU." From Selfies to Stories, news feeds to podcasts, building a professional personification, an "image", or a brand that depicts YOU as the expert and Go-To person in your profession, is the end goal.

But, in the age of "It's all about YOU", I feel there is need to take pause and remind you that perhaps, it is not. Allow me to explain.

Approximately 52 years ago, Neil Armstrong and Apollo 11 landed on the moon. Not a single proud American who can recall that moment doesn't associate Neil for that landmark accomplishment. But let's be honest. The great Neil Armstrong did not land on the moon by himself. There is no doubt that as he took that one small step as a man, there was a mankind support team behind him.

Which brings me to the point of this article. As a Realtor, where one part of our job is to establish our self as a leader in our field, where is the fine line between recognizing those who helped you reach your moon? And if we do recognize their efforts, does it make us any less of a professional if we give credit to a great team/company that stands behind us?

My answer is "No." However, the balance is found in incorporating subtle yet professional reminders into our daily business practices that creates a healthy balance between the promotion of Self and the gratitude of Support. I call it the 6 Steps of Great Agents who Remember the WHO in their career. It looks like this:

1: **Great Agents Create a Team.**

The universal Law of Creation proves that the combined effort of many is much more effective than the sole effort of one. Therefore, a great agent understands the importance of creating a team or being part of a team/company. But not just a team of random individuals. It is a team with a synergy, vision, slogan and name and a specific seat on the team bus.

2: **Great Agents recognize their team.**

Certainly, it is not professional to place an Acknowledgement List on every full-page ad. And we all know it would look silly to list our entire team by name in our social media. That said however, you can hashtag your team name and team slogan, and by doing so, you recognize everyone who has contributed to your success. #Surterre

3. **Great agents make their team feel visible, every day.**

Great agents take the time to make each of their team members visible. This means, addressing them by name, making eye contact when they have questions, developing a habit of going out of your way to say hello, and acknowledge them in words and writing when they do a good job.

4. **Great agents show their appreciation by Acts of Service.**

Great agents make a point to show their appreciation by investing back into their team. This can include small gestures such as buying lunch or providing pastries on a scheduled date every week or month. Or this can mean holiday bonuses, or small gift cards for birthdays. Always keep in mind that your team makes a very small fraction of what you do, yet their contribution is immense. And small Acts of Service is a big way to offer on-going recognition.

5. Great agents are team players themselves who live by example.

Great agents not only pay recognition forward to their team, but they are also pay it upward. Meaning, they show by example, recognition to the company that invested in them first. Without that investment we might no be where we are today in our career.

6. Great agents take the right time to publicly say thank you.

And then at the end of the day, a great agent sometimes takes the *right* opportunity to publicly thank the important members of their team in writing at landmark moments. Which at this point, I would like to use this platform to thank Surterre Properties and their amazing staff and leadership and my excellent PR Agency, Sterling Publications, Paula Steuer and her team, for creating this opportunity for me to have MY real estate voice heard in Inman. I realize that statement did come back to the "ME factor." Yet I know I wouldn't be here, without you.

Soul...the essence of all we are and do

Chapter 27

BE THE REALTOR WITH A "SOUL"

As many of you know, I'm passionate about "Raising the Bar" on our Real Estate profession, and I'm on a mission to put the "Soul" back into our industry. The reason I'm focused on the "Soul of Real Estate" is that truthfully speaking, I think our profession can use a little more of the sensitive stuff.

As a 30-year veteran in the industry, I have learned a valuable lesson throughout my career. I've learned that in light of the generous commissions we make and the freedom we experience in our profession, we Realtors are in actuality, entrusted with a *great* responsibility. That responsibility being the selling or acquiring of a person's most valued possession, which is their home. Home, where they will raise their children. Home, where they will create a lifetime of memories. Home, where they will get their first pet, broken arm, lose a loved one, or where the next big idea might be birthed from their garage office.

> Soul (n): "the moral and emotional nature of human beings"

As industry professionals, it's important to remember that though the seduction of the commission can entice us all (especially in the great O. C., where millions of dollars a year are up for grabs), Real Estate is more than just the game of making money. Meaning, where we repetitively make our livelihood by moving from one transaction to the next, our clients are often investing their *life's* savings. Where we are looking at the *art* of the deal that will "close in a matter of weeks," our clients are looking at their investment as potential memories of their life to come. Or, where we are looking outward to find our next client that will make us our next commission, they will look back and remember us as the ones who helped them find their "home." In other words, the art of the Real Estate transaction is not just about the transfer of bricks and mortar, and the hardline details in the contract. It is instead an *intimate* transaction where we must never forget what I call the "Soul" of the transaction, which in my opinion means the mind, will and emotion behind every deal.

Reality Check:
Clients needs come before all others.

Specifically, this means:

1. Being *Mindful* of your client's needs and limitations. Or in other words, it's having the maturity to remember that behind every transaction is a *real* person, and our job is to meet their needs as though they are our own.

2. Respecting their *Will*, which is their power and freedom of choice. As we all know, some clients move quickly. Some do *not*. Some know what they want. Some need to see every option on the market before they can decide. Our job is to have patience and respect for our client's individual timing and to ride that boat as long as *they* need.

3. Finally, it means honoring their *Emotions,* which as my wife always says, "are not up for negotiation." As Soul-Sensitive agents, we must remember that there are certain things in the deal that we

cannot control or change. One of those is how or *why* our clients "feel" a certain way about any part of the process. As professionals, our job is *not* to judge how our clients feel. Our job is to find the deal that will make them *feel good* about working with us all while making their investment of a lifetime.

If I had to sum up my "Soul-bar" into one final thought, I would say this: In our Real-Estate world where social media, glossy eight-page brochures, and fancy videos are our primary tools to attract clients, I want to challenge you this season to add the element of Soul to your presentation packages. The reason is because in this competitive market where all the pomp and circumstance of promotion is available to every agent, it's the word-of-mouth and personal referral that will put your name in front of all the rest.

May the "Soul" be with you…

About the Author

Recognized as an industry innovator and thought leader in the world of real estate, Spyro Kemble has earned a reputation for excellence. Having cultivated a network of prestigious alliances with some of the most in-demand organizations, brands, and influencers across the globe, Spyro's tenure and insight have proven to be invaluable both personally and professionally. As a trusted advisor for both peers and clientele, Spyro's commitment to upholding the gold standard in all he does is relentless. His unwavering dedication has allowed him to flourish throughout the ebbs and flows in real estate, having closed nearly half a billion dollars in sales in his career which has spanned more than 30 years. Today, he enjoys being able to mentor future generations and serve on distinguished advisory boards such as the Newport Beach Association of Realtors and the Orange County Sherriff Department's Advisory Council. Additionally, Spyro shares his expertise with real estate professionals across the nation as a featured speaker at industry driven conferences like the C.A.R. Expo, and as a Contributing Writer to Inman.com. He is a former President of the Newport Beach Association of Realtors, and is a featured speaker at the Inman Luxury Conference.

With a passion for life and a keen eye that appreciates the finer things, his energy, quick wit and relatability have created a platform for him in the public eye, through the Bravo TV show "Real Estate Wars". His most recent media endeavor includes the launch of his own podcast show, as well as the release of his first book entitled Reality Check: Lessons Learned, Candor and Consequence. Married to the love of his life Tracy, and residing in Newport Beach with their beloved Samoyed "Habibi", Spyro enjoys living and working in beautiful, coastal Orange County, California. Together, Tracy and Spyro are active philanthropists for the W.I.N Foundation, a non-profit organization which seeks to provide assistance to abused women while fostering self-esteem recovery. Spyro currently serves as a Board Member for the W.I.N. Foundation in addition to his work with the Maryam Parman Foundation for Injured Children, Inc.

Having attended UCLA, studying economics and finance, Spyro is a proud Bruin fan. In college, he was on the wrestling team where his competitive nature was sharpened. In his free time, Spyro can often be found enjoying a fine cigar, glass of scotch, and throughout the year at his vacation home in the Greek Isles.

www.ingramcontent.com/pod-product-compliance
Lightning Source LLC
Chambersburg PA
CBHW052258220526
45471CB00001B/396